Hymns in commemoration of the sufferings of our blessed Saviour Jesus Christ, compos'd for the celebration of his holy supper. By Joseph Stennett. The third edition enlarged.

Joseph Stennett

PRINT EDITIONS

Eighteenth Century
Collections Online
Print Editions

Gale ECCO Print Editions

Relive history with *Eighteenth Century Collections Online*, now available in print for the independent historian and collector. This series includes the most significant English-language and foreign-language works printed in Great Britain during the eighteenth century, and is organized in seven different subject areas including literature and language; medicine, science, and technology; and religion and philosophy. The collection also includes thousands of important works from the Americas.

The eighteenth century has been called "The Age of Enlightenment." It was a period of rapid advance in print culture and publishing, in world exploration, and in the rapid growth of science and technology – all of which had a profound impact on the political and cultural landscape. At the end of the century the American Revolution, French Revolution and Industrial Revolution, perhaps three of the most significant events in modern history, set in motion developments that eventually dominated world political, economic, and social life.

In a groundbreaking effort, Gale initiated a revolution of its own: digitization of epic proportions to preserve these invaluable works in the largest online archive of its kind. Contributions from major world libraries constitute over 175,000 original printed works. Scanned images of the actual pages, rather than transcriptions, recreate the works *as they first appeared.*

Now for the first time, these high-quality digital scans of original works are available via print-on-demand, making them readily accessible to libraries, students, independent scholars, and readers of all ages.

For our initial release we have created seven robust collections to form one the world's most comprehensive catalogs of 18th century works.

Initial Gale ECCO Print Editions collections include:

History and Geography
Rich in titles on English life and social history, this collection spans the world as it was known to eighteenth-century historians and explorers. Titles include a wealth of travel accounts and diaries, histories of nations from throughout the world, and maps and charts of a world that was still being discovered. Students of the War of American Independence will find fascinating accounts from the British side of conflict.

Social Science

Delve into what it was like to live during the eighteenth century by reading the first-hand accounts of everyday people, including city dwellers and farmers, businessmen and bankers, artisans and merchants, artists and their patrons, politicians and their constituents. Original texts make the American, French, and Industrial revolutions vividly contemporary.

Medicine, Science and Technology

Medical theory and practice of the 1700s developed rapidly, as is evidenced by the extensive collection, which includes descriptions of diseases, their conditions, and treatments. Books on science and technology, agriculture, military technology, natural philosophy, even cookbooks, are all contained here.

Literature and Language

Western literary study flows out of eighteenth-century works by Alexander Pope, Daniel Defoe, Henry Fielding, Frances Burney, Denis Diderot, Johann Gottfried Herder, Johann Wolfgang von Goethe, and others. Experience the birth of the modern novel, or compare the development of language using dictionaries and grammar discourses.

Religion and Philosophy

The Age of Enlightenment profoundly enriched religious and philosophical understanding and continues to influence present-day thinking. Works collected here include masterpieces by David Hume, Immanuel Kant, and Jean-Jacques Rousseau, as well as religious sermons and moral debates on the issues of the day, such as the slave trade. The Age of Reason saw conflict between Protestantism and Catholicism transformed into one between faith and logic -- a debate that continues in the twenty-first century.

Law and Reference

This collection reveals the history of English common law and Empire law in a vastly changing world of British expansion. Dominating the legal field is the *Commentaries of the Law of England* by Sir William Blackstone, which first appeared in 1765. Reference works such as almanacs and catalogues continue to educate us by revealing the day-to-day workings of society.

Fine Arts

The eighteenth-century fascination with Greek and Roman antiquity followed the systematic excavation of the ruins at Pompeii and Herculaneum in southern Italy; and after 1750 a neoclassical style dominated all artistic fields. The titles here trace developments in mostly English-language works on painting, sculpture, architecture, music, theater, and other disciplines. Instructional works on musical instruments, catalogs of art objects, comic operas, and more are also included.

The BiblioLife Network

This project was made possible in part by the BiblioLife Network (BLN), a project aimed at addressing some of the huge challenges facing book preservationists around the world. The BLN includes libraries, library networks, archives, subject matter experts, online communities and library service providers. We believe every book ever published should be available as a high-quality print reproduction; printed on-demand anywhere in the world. This insures the ongoing accessibility of the content and helps generate sustainable revenue for the libraries and organizations that work to preserve these important materials.

The following book is in the "public domain" and represents an authentic reproduction of the text as printed by the original publisher. While we have attempted to accurately maintain the integrity of the original work, there are sometimes problems with the original work or the micro-film from which the books were digitized. This can result in minor errors in reproduction. Possible imperfections include missing and blurred pages, poor pictures, markings and other reproduction issues beyond our control. Because this work is culturally important, we have made it available as part of our commitment to protecting, preserving, and promoting the world's literature.

GUIDE TO FOLD-OUTS MAPS and OVERSIZED IMAGES

The book you are reading was digitized from microfilm captured over the past thirty to forty years. Years after the creation of the original microfilm, the book was converted to digital files and made available in an online database.

In an online database, page images do not need to conform to the size restrictions found in a printed book. When converting these images back into a printed bound book, the page sizes are standardized in ways that maintain the detail of the original. For large images, such as fold-out maps, the original page image is split into two or more pages

Guidelines used to determine how to split the page image follows:

• Some images are split vertically; large images require vertical and horizontal splits.
• For horizontal splits, the content is split left to right.
• For vertical splits, the content is split from top to bottom.
• For both vertical and horizontal splits, the image is processed from top left to bottom right.

844
1 5

HYMNS

In Commemoration

Of the SUFFERINGS

OF

Our Blessed Saviour

JESUS CHRIST,

Compós'd

For the CELEBRATION of his

Holy Supper.

By JOSEPH STENNETT.

The Third Edition Enlarged.

Mat. 26. 30. *And when they had sung an Hymn they went out to the Mount of Olives.*

LONDON, Printed by *J. Darby* in *Bartholomew Close*, for *N. Cliff* and *D. Jackson*, at the *Bible* and *Three Crowns* in *Cheapside*, near *Mercers-Chapel.* 1713.

WHEREAS our Saviour inftituted the Sacrament of his Body and Blood to be a perpetual Memorial of his Death, and concluded the fame by Singing an Hymn together with his Difciples; his Authority and Example are fufficient to oblige us to do fo likewife.

And that this Duty may be perform'd with an humble Reverence of the Divine Majefty, and a deep Contrition for our numerous Sins, with Faith in the Affiftance of the Holy Spirit, and fteddy Refolution of Obedience to all the Laws of Jefus Chrift; We recommend the following Hymns, the Defign and Performance of which render them very proper to raife fuch Affections in us, as are futable to fo folemn an Occafion.

A 2   To

To which may be added the Version of *Solomon's Song*, by the same Author; whereby we may arrive at a Knowledg of the Meaning of that Divine Poem, and which may serve to excite becoming Affections in our Minds on other Occasions.

Jos. *Maisters*,   Dan. *Williams*,
John *Shower*,   Rich. *Allen*,
Tho. *Reynolds*.   John *Piggott*,
Will. *Harris*,   John *Foxon*,
Jabez *Earle*,   Benj. *Grosvenor*,
Sam *Rosewel*,   Nat. *Hodges*,
Tho. *Bradbury*,   Eben. *Wilson*.
Benj. *Stinton*.

A N

AN

ADVERTISEMENT

TO THE

ʹREADER.

MANY of the following Hymns were compos'd only for the Ufe of the Congregation under my peculiar Charge, but by means of the Copies taken by fome Perfons who heard them dictated in Publick, they were difpers'd into many Hands.

To hinder the Propagation of thofe Miftakes that flide into Copies haftily written, and which are multiplied by being often tranfcrib'd from different Hands, and to oblige thofe of my Friends who defir'd perfect Copies for themfelves, and who endeavour'd to perfuade me they would be accepta-

A 3 *ble*

ble and useful to many other Congregations, I consented to make 'em publick.

The two first Impressions being gone off, and a third for some time desir'd; I thought meet to review them, that I might render them less imperfect, by correcting them in several places, which I have done, as well as added a few Hymns not publish'd before

I have prescrib'd to my self, in the Composition of them all, to keep the Cross of Christ continually in View ∙ seeing his Holy Supper is design'd evidently to set him forth before our Eyes, crucified among us. I have endeavour'd to assist the Devotion of those who communicate at his Sacred Table, by suggesting what I thought most proper to dispose 'em to Humility and Repentance, to Faith and Hope, to Admiration and Joy, to Love and Gratitude. And tho the Matter of 'em, as well as the Expression, may seem very much diversified, so that some of them are much more directly adapted to excite this or that pious Affection or Christian Virtue than others, yet they are

gene-

generally so order'd as to have an obvious regard to them all.

I have cited those Scriptures in the Margin from whence the Thoughts, and frequently the very Words, are taken; by which means the Reader, if he is pleas'd to turn to the Passages refer'd to, may easy explain to himself those Phrases and Allusions, which at the first glance appear somewhat hard and obscure.

I have chosen those Measures which fit the Tunes in most common Use among us; tho they are not very favourable to a Vein of Poesy. It being impossible to express the Sense so elegantly, when 'tis cramp'd and confin'd to very short Lines, as when a larger Scope is allow'd.

I have carefully avoided those very bold Flights and those Heathenish Phrases which some have indulg'd even in Divine Poesy; for I cannot think 'em consistent with the Gravity, Purity, and Perspicuity which ought to be preserv'd in Hymns calculated for the immediate Service of God,
and

A 4

and for the common Edification of Christians.

And because some few Words that are less common here and there occur, where some plainer Word as expressive of the Sense, or as grateful to the Ear, did not present; lest these should amuse any Reader, and render some Passages difficult to him, I have subjoin'd a Table at the End to explain those Terms, that Persons of a mean Capacity, and not conversant with other Writings besides those of the Bible, or some plain Books of Devotion, might be able to sing these Hymns with Understanding.

They who reflect on what I have already said, will make considerable Allowances for the Defects they find in the Poetry. And perhaps the Imperfection of this Essay may be an Occasion of setting some better Hand to work, to oblige the Publick with politer Compositions of this kind.

The Love of Truth, and a charitable Regard to some very serious and pious Christians, whose Minds have been so perplext with Scruples about the Law-
fulness

fulnefs of Singing in the Service of
God, that they wholly omit this fo
very ufeful and agreeable part of Divine Worfhip, mov'd me to defire
a very Worthy and Ingenious Friend
to prefix to this Book of Hymns fome
Arguments on that Subject, with the
Subftance of which he had before entertain'd me, in giving me an Account
how thofe Prejudices againft finging
of Pfalms, &c himfelf was formerly
under, had been remov'd.

His Friendfhip, and the Hope I endeavour'd to make him conceive that
what had convinc'd him, might (by
the Bleffing of God) have the fame
effect on fome other Perfons under
the like Circumftances, made him
willing not to refufe my Requeft, tho
he has not given me the Liberty of
mentioning his Name.

To this Edition I have alfo prefix'd a fhort Effay in Verfe by way of
Dedication to our BLESSED SA-
VIOUR, to whom thefe Hymns of
right belong, as being confecrated to
the Service of his Holy Table.

If

If any thing I have attempted ſhall redound to the Glory of his ſacred Name, and to the ſpiritual Advantage of any part of his Church ; as I ſhall account it an Honour, ſo it will be an Occaſion of Joy and Satisfaction to me.

J. S.

THE

THE
PREFACE,

By Another Hand.

I HAVE at the requeſt of the Reverend Author, prefix'd this brief Diſcourſe to the following Hymns, in vindication of the Practice of ſinging the Praiſes of God, as a part of Chriſtian Worſhip. And I the more readily comply'd, becauſe I have my ſelf labour'd under the Prejudices of Education to the contrary; till convinc'd of what I now eſteem my Duty, by the higheſt Authority, *viz.* That of Chriſt and his Apoſtles.

I will not doubt of a becoming Reception from thoſe Chriſtians who have different Sentiments; I ſhall only intreat the Favour, not to ſay Juſtice, of any ſuch who ſhall read this Preface, to think it poſſible for them to have been miſtaken, and to be equally willing to receive the Truth, on which
ſoever

.soever side of the Question it shall appear to be.

One that reads over the New Testament with any attention, must observe a frequent Mention of *singing Psalms, and Hymns, and spiritual Songs.*

The Evangelists * *Matthew* and *Mark* both inform us, that our blessed Saviour, together with his Disciples, *sung an Hymn* at the conclusion of the Lord's Supper, then instituted a standing Ordinance in the Church.

St. *Luke* in his History of the Acts of the Apostles tells us, that *Paul* and *Silas* being in Prison, and having been scourg'd on account of their Ministry, at *midnight pray'd and sung Praises to God,* so that *the Prisoners heard them.*

Acts 16. 25.

The Apostle *Paul* reproving the *Corinthians* for a vain Ostentation of their Gifts, particularly that of speaking in foreign Languages, tells † them, that they ought to *sing with Under-*

---

* Mat 26. 30. *and* Mark 14. 26. *And when they had sung an Hymn, &c.*

† 1 Cor 14. 15. *I will sing with the Spirit, and I will sing with the Understanding also.*

standing ;

ftanding; which could not be, whilſt they were ignorant of the Language ſung, tho it might be underſtood by the *Precentor*, or Perſon who dictated to the reſt.

The ſame Apoſtle exhorts both the * *Epheſians*. and † *Coloſſians* to ſing Pſalms, and Hymns, and Spiritual Songs.

The Apoſtle ‖ *James* alſo exhorts the ſcatter'd Chriſtians of the twelve Tribes to whom he writes, to expreſs their Joy on all occaſions by *ſinging Pſalmᵉ* of Praiſe to God.

---

* Epheſ. 5. 19, 20. *Speaking to your ſelves in Pſalms, and Hymns, and Spiritual Songs; ſinging and making melody in your Hearts to the Lord; giving thanks always for all things to God and the Father, in the name of our Lord Jeſus Chriſt*

† Coloſ. 3. 16, 17. *Let the Word of God dwell in you richly in all Wiſdom, teaching and admoniſhing one another in Pſalms, and Hymns, and Spiritual Songs, ſinging with Grace in your Hearts to the Lord. And whatſoever ye do in Word or in Deed, do all in the Name of the Lrd Jeſus, giving Thanks to God and the Father by him.*

‖ James 5. 13. *Is any among you afflicted? let him pray. Is any merry? let him ſing Pſalms.*

Now

Now what is to be collected from
all these Examples, Precepts, and *Re-*
gulations of this Practice, but that
singing the Praises of God is a part
of Divine Worship in the Christian
Church? And certainly any one
would make this Conclusion from
reading these Passages, who had never heard of any Controversy about
it. It is indeed possible to raise Ob-
jections against any thing · Gramma-
tical Criticisms may be pretended,
and a forc'd Construction may be put
on the plainest Words; but if the
same Rules be allow'd for the Interpretation of Scripture in general as
must be made use of to evade the
Force of the Texts I have mention'd,
the plainest Precepts may be render'd doubtful, and the clearest Doc-
trines overthrown. However, since
there are some who still remain un-
convinc'd of this Duty, I shall endeavour, without stating them particularly, to obviate all their Ob-
jections, and confirm the Truth, by
shewing,

1. That the Singing mention'd in
the several recited Texts is Proper.

2. That it was practis'd as a part of
Divine Worship.

3. That

3. That it was perform'd by joint Voices.

1. That the Singing mention'd in the several recited Texts, must be understood in a proper, and not a metaphorical sense. To this there can no Objection be made, but from some pretended Criticism on the Original: for every one that understands *English*, knows that *to sing* is to express Words with a tuneable Voice, according to the Rules of Musick; as proper *Speaking* is to express Words according to the Rules of Grammar: both being to be perform'd by Imitation and Practice, without an Acquaintance with the Theory of either; for they are equally natural, tho both reducible to artificial Rules. *Singing* in English is taken in no other sense, nor can any bare *English* Reader doubt whether this be the meaning.

As to the Original, the Word made use of by the * Evangelists is deriv'd from a Verb whose pri-

---

* Mat. 26. 30. Ὑμνήσαντες.
  Mark 14. 30. Ὑμνήσαντες.
  Acts 16. 25. Ὕμνεν.

mary

mary Signification is *to sing an Hymn*
or Song of Praise.

Sometimes indeed it is taken absolute-
ly *to Praise*, without determining the
manner. But this is a certain Rule in the
Interpretation of all Writings, to take
Words in their first and most proper
Signification, unless some good reason be
assign'd why, that Sense cannot be admitted in the Place in question. Now in
the Instances under consideration no
such reason can be produc'd, and therefore it ought to be render'd, as in our
Translation, they *sung* an Hymn or
Song of Praise.

In the Epistle to the * *Corinthians*,
and that of † St. *James*, the Word
us'd in the Original signifies properly
to sing. It is also sometimes us'd for
singing to or playing on a musical
Instrument, but when apply'd to the
Voice, is never taken in any other sense
than that of strictly *Singing.* In the
Epistle to the ‖ *Colossians* we find another Word which also signifies pro-

---

* 1 Cor. 14. 15. Ψαλῶ τῷ πνεύμαϊ,
ψαλῶ δὲ ᾖ τῷ νοΐ.

† James 5. 1. Εὐθυμεῖ τις, ψαλλ τω.

‖ Col. 3. 15. Ἄδοντες

perly

perly to fing, but is fometimes us'd to
exprefs the writing a Poem or Copy of
Verfes; which is a Senfe of the Word
that I fuppofe no body will contend
for in this place, and befides which no
other Senfe can be put on the Word,
but that of proper *Singing.*

In the Epiftle to the * *Ephefians*
both the Words laft mention'd are
made ufe of. So that had St. *Paul*
ever fo much defign'd to fpeak of proper Singing, it was impoffible for him
by Words to have exprefs'd himfelf
more clearly and determinately.

All this, I think, amounts to a full
proof, that our Tranflation is in this
matter every where juft, and that
proper Singing is fpoken of in all the
Inftances given. As to the particular
Tunes in which the Words are to be
exprefs'd, they are left as much at
liberty as the Tone or different Ele-
vation and Accenting the Voice in
Speaking. Decency is the only Limi-
tation, and as the Tone of the Voice
ought not to be wanton and ludi-
crous, fo neither fhould the Mufical
Tunes be light and airy· both ought

---

* Eph. 5. 19. 'Αδ̓ο̃ιες ϗ ϕάλλονιες.

in Divine Worſhip to be grave and
ſolemn, becoming our Addreſſes to
God

2. That this Singing mention'd in
the ſeveral recited Texts was perform'd and enjoin'd as a part of Divine Worſhip

The Euchariſtical Hymn perform'd
by our Lord and his Apoſtles, is acknowledg'd, even by thoſe who deny
that it was ſung, to have been an Act
of Praiſe and Thankſgiving to God
For it is agreed on all ſides, that
Hymning is praiſing, whether by Song
or without , and to be ſure God was
the Object with whom they were then
converſant.

In the Inſtance of *Paul* and *Silas*
the Words are expreſs, *They ſung
Praiſes unto God.*

To the *Epheſians* the Apoſtle thus
expreſſes it : *Speaking to your ſelves
in Pſalms and Hymns, and ſpiritual
Songs, ſinging and making melody in
your Hearts to the Lord , giving Thanks
always for all things unto God and the
Father, in the Name of our Lord Jeſus
Chriſt.* And to the *Coloſſians* he ſays,
in almoſt the ſame words *Let the
Word of God dwell in you richly in all
Wiſdom, teaching and admoniſhing one
                                  another*

another in Pfalms and Hymns, and fpi-
ritual Songs; finging with Grace in your
Hearts to the Lord: and whatfoever ye
do in word or deed, do all in the Name
of the Lord Jefus, giving Thanks to
God and the Father by him. In both
which places we may obferve the
Action, *giving Thanks* or Praife; the
Object, *God, thro the Mediator,* and
the external Mode, *Singing.*

The Apoftle *James* has it : *Is any* Jam. 5 13.
among you afflicted, let him pray? Is
any merry, let him fing Pfalms?
which amounts to thus much : That
as Prayer is a proper manner of expreffing our Wants and Griefs to
God, fo is Singing a proper way of
expreffing our Joy and Gratitude.
And indeed Mufick and Poetry are
both proper to exprefs and move the
Paffions. They heighten and improve
the Affections of Love and Joy,
whilft they gently calm the uneafy
Senfations of Grief and Sorrow. Thus
we find the Royal Pfalmift finging one
while lofty Hymns of Praife, anon a
mournful penitential Song, and again
fervent Prayers and Supplications for
needful Bleffings. So that nothing
which is fit to be addrefs'd to God,
can be unfit to be fung before him.

What

1 Cor. 14. 15.

What St. *Paul* says of this matter to the *Corinthians*; *I will sing with the Spirit, and I will sing with Understanding also*; plainly appears to be spoke of the publick Worship in the Church, being join'd with Prayer, which had suffer'd the same Abuse with Singing from the Vanity and Affectation of some in the Church, who had receiv'd the Gift of Tongues, and prided themselves in speaking before the People in an unknown Language: whereas they ought both to pray and to sing the Praises of God in such a Tongue, as that all present might understand, and join in the same Act of Worship with a sincere Devotion and a due Knowledg.

Now from what has been said under this Head it appears, That in all the recited places Singing is spoken of as being perform'd to God as the immediate Object: which is all that is necessary to constitute any Action Religious, or a part of Divine Worship.

3 I now come to shew that singing the Praises of God was perform'd by the conjoint Voices of several Persons together. It is said of our Lord and his Disciples, by both *Matthew* and *Mark*

Mark, That *they sung* an Hymn [in the plural number] whereas Chriſt's bleſſing the Bread, and giving thanks when he took the Cup, are both expreſs'd [in the ſingular number] as perform'd by Chriſt ſpeaking ſingly, and the reſt joining mentally only. And that they did ſo join with Chriſt in that Action, I ſuppoſe no body doubts; tho it be ſaid, *He gave thanks and he bleſſed*, that is, he in the name of them all, and on their behalf as well as for himſelf, ſolemnly pronounc'd their joint Supplications and Thankſgivings to God. But here the Phraſe is alter'd, and the Evangeliſts tell us, That *they ſung an Hymn*; that is, with joint Voices, as well as with united Hearts. Which as it is the plain and obvious meaning of the Expreſſion, ſo there can no other reaſon be aſſign'd for the Variation of the Phraſe.

St. *Luke* tells us, that the Priſoners heard *Paul* and *Silas* both performing their joint Devotions to God. I ſuppoſe no body imagines they pronounc'd their Prayers together. It muſt therefore be the Praiſes which they ſung jointly, and that with a Voice ſo rais'd, as that their Fellow Prisoners heard them.

There is another Passage in the History of the Acts, which I think, if duly consider'd, is to this purpose. In the *4th* Chapter and *24th* Verse it is said, That *they* [*i. e* the Apostles that were then at *Jerusalem*, and the Believers that consorted with them, being assembled together] *lift up their Voice to God with one accord, and said*, *&c.* From the Context it appears, that the Worship then offer'd was a solemn Thanksgiving (tho concluded with a Petition) and that on a very eminent occasion, the Deliverance of *Peter* and *John* from the Rage of the *Sanhedrim*, by whom, after Examination, they were dismiss'd without Punishment, and this in accomplishment of *David's* Prophecy, *Psalm* 2 1. Now the matter being Praise and Thanksgiving, and that express'd with united Voice as well as Heart, I see no room to doubt but that it was perform'd as an Hymn or sacred Song : unless it should be thought that they pronounc'd a bare Oration with united Voices, which is a sense I believe none ever yet contended for. We no where read of a Prayer's being pronounc'd by joint Voices, but of

Praises

Praises being sung by joint Voices
I have already given Instances. And
the Action here being solemn Praise
offer'd up by joint Voices, tho it be
not said *they sung,* yet it is more
than probable that they did sing, for
tho all *saying* (which is the Word
us'd) be not *singing,* yet to be sure all
singing is *saying.*

These Instances, I think, are suffi-
cient to prove that singing by con-
join'd Voices was practis'd in the
Christian Church.

The Sum of what has been said, is,
That from divers Texts of Scripture,
collected out of the New Testament,
it does appear, that the Praises of
God were sung by conjoint Voices
in the Christian Church, as a part
of Divine Worship, and that this
Duty is on several occasions regulated,
injoin'd and recommended to the several Churches to whom the Apo
stles wrote their Epistles From all
this it naturally follows, that it is
now the Duty of all Christians to
sing the Praises of God, both in their
publick Assemblys, and in their more
private religious Exercises.

To

To this Account from Scripture, I shall add one foreign Testimony to prove that it was the constant Practice of the primitive Christians, in their religious Assemblys, to sing with conjoint Voices, Hymns or Songs of Praise to Christ as God   And that is of *Pliny* the younger who was Governour of all *Pontus*, and *Bithynia* in *Asia Minor*, together with the City of *Byzantium*, not as an ordinary Proconsul, but as the Emperor's immediate Lieutenant with extraordinary Power. This great Man had for some time, in obedience to his Master's Commands, exercis'd his Authority in a vigorous Prosecution of the Christians, but finding that if he proceeded to punish all that acknowledg'd themselves Christians, he must in a manner lay waste his Provinces, he thought it necessary to write a Letter to the Emperor himself about this matter. wherein after having given a particular account of his Procedure against the Christians, and of their Obstinacy in persisting to Death, and of the great Numbers that had embrac'd this new Superstition, as he calls it, he relates what upon Examination he had found to be the Sum of the Christian Practice,

Practice *They affirm'd, says he, that the whole sum of that Offence or Error lay in this, that they were wont on a set day to meet together before Sun-rise, and to sing together a Hymn to Christ as a God, and oblige themselves by a Sacrament not to commit any Wickedness, but to abstain from Theft, Robbery, Adultery, to keep Faith, and to restore any Pledg intrusted with them; and after that they retir'd, and met again at a common Meal, in which was nothing extraordinary or criminal.* This Epistle was written to *Trajan* then Emperor, about 71 Years after the Death of our blessed Saviour, *Ann. Dom.* 104. and in the 7*th* Year of *Trajan's* Reign. By this unquestionable Authority we see what

* Affirmabant autem hanc fuisse summam vel Culpæ suæ, vel Erroris, quod essent soliti stato die ante lucem convenire, carmenque Christo, quasi Deo, dicere secum invicem; seque Sacramento non in Scelus aliquod obstringere, sed ne Furta, ne Latrocinia, ne Adulteria committerent, ne fidem fallerent, ne depositum appellari abnegarent: quibus peractis morem sibi discedendi fuisse, rursusque coeundi ad capiendum Cibum promiscuum tamen & innoxium. *Plin. Ep. lib.* 10. *Ep.* 97.

account

account the Chriſtians of that time gave of their own Practice, *viz.* That in their religious Aſſemblies they ſung Songs or Hymns to *Jeſus Chriſt* as God.

Concerning the following Compoſures I ſhall only ſay, that the Subjects are well choſen, and admirably adapted to the Occaſion, proper to excite becoming Affections at that great Feaſt of Love, the Lord's Supper, inſtituted in commemoration of that perfect Sacrifice, by which alone we are deliver'd from everlaſting Deſtruction, and intitled to eternal Bleſſedneſs. The Poetry is chaſt and polite, the Expreſſion clear and juſt, in every reſpect becoming the noble Theme As ſuch I recommend it both to the Publick and Private Uſe of thoſe devout Chriſtians, whoſe Breaſts are warm'd by a heavenly Fire, and whoſe Souls are tranſported with a lively Senſe of Divine Love.

A

A HYMN,

Written by the same Hand, upon his being convinc'd that *Singing* is a part of Divine Worship.

ETERNAL intellectual Light,
  With pure Illapse my Mind inspire;
And whilst I sing Thee great and bright,
Inflame my Breast with Heav'nly Fire.

Tho long mistaken, I withheld
Harmonious Song divine, thy Due;
Yet better Knowledg now instill'd,
Thy tuneful Praise my Voice shall shew.

Substantial Glory, from thy Throne
Around diffus'd, illumines Heaven;
With Life and Love fills ev'ry one,
To whom those happy Seats are given.

Nor there confin'd, thy Beams divine
Irradia   all thy Church below:
Thy Chosen with thy Brightness shine,
And by their Love, thy Grace they show.

To

To every Heart, by secret Ways
Convey'd, Mysterious Influence !
The bright Effusion of thy Rays,
Gives Knowledg, Truth and Innocence.

When in deep Trouble, and opprest,
Thy consolating Light sustains
Thy drooping Saints; tho sore distrest,
Calm Peace and Joy succeed their Pains.

So the returning Summer's Sun
Does with fresh Vigor bright appear;
The Clouds dispell'd, the Winter gon,
Glad Plenty crowns the smiling Year.

THE

THE

DEDICATION.

O THOU whom Angels with their
  Hymns addreſs !
 To whom all Knees muſt bow, all
  Tongues confeſs !
Sacred to THEE, this Sacrifice of Praiſe
A willing Hand upon thy Altar lay's,
Encourag'd by that Goodneſs which approves
A poor Man's Gift, tho but a Pair of Doves.
May I have one accepting Smile from Thee,
'Tis more than all the World's Applauſe to me.
        Happy !

Happy ! if I a contrite Spirit bring,

And feel my Breaſt warm'd with the Love I
    ſing ;

Happy ! if theſe my Songs ſucceſsful prove

To make one Sinner look on Thee, and love ;

To make one Prodigal confeſs thy Charms,

And fly for Pardon to thy dying Arms ;

To fan their pious Flame who Thee adore,

And make the Souls that love Thee, love Thee
    more ;

Make 'em their Praiſes and their Vows renew,

And give their All to Thee, to whom all Hearts
    are due.

                       (Way,

   LORD, what a Train of Woes attend thy

From dark *Gethſemanè* to *Golgotha* !

What gloomy Terrors did conſpire to roll

Through all th' Apartments of thy inmoſt Soul !

What Troubles in thy lab'ring Boſom met,

And flow'd in Tears, flow'd in a bloody Sweat !

What Clouds with Thunder charg'd, black
    Horror ſpread !

And broke in Storms of Vengeance on thy Head !

                      This

This difmal Night a darker Morn portends ;

Seiz'd by thy Foes, abandon'd by thy Friends ;

By one of them abjur'd, by one betray'd,

And with a treacherous Kifs a Pris'ner made :

From one Tribunal to another led,

New Pretexts fought thy facred Blood to fhed :

Charg'd with thofe Crimes thy righteous Soul
   abhor'd,

And there condemn'd where thou fhould'ft be
   ador'd

Humble and meek the paffive Victim ftands,

By vileft Tongues blafphem'd, and ftruck by
   rudeft Hands.

A Prince to Univerfal Empire born,

Scepters his Hand, and Crowns his Head had
   worn,

Now holds a Reed, and wears a Wreath of
   Thorn.

The favage Croud the King of Glory jeers,

With loud Reproaches wound his patient
   Ears,

And mix their foaming Spittle with his
   Tears.

And

And now with flow and feeble Pace I try

To trace thy Footſteps up Mount *Calvary*;

There ſee thoſe Hands, that made and ſcatter'd Bread,

And Thouſands with the growing Banquet fed,

Thoſe Hands that heal'd the Sick, and rais'd
the Dead;

That oft returning Sinners did embrace,

And for them oft implor'd forgiving Grace,

With pious Ardor lifted up to Heaven,

Now pierc'd with Nails amid their Sinews
driven:

Thy ſacred Feet the ſame rude Treatment know,

And both in purple Streams their Torment ſhow.

I ſee that Face which Angels bow'd before,

Clouded with Sorrow, bath'd in Sweat and Gore,

Thoſe Eyes that, mov'd with pity, did condole

The various Woes of every human Soul,

And ſtain'd their Luſtre with their pious Streams,

In ſhades of Death now quench their ſetting Beams

With cruel Men the Powers of Hell below

The laſt Efforts of active Malice ſhow,

And at thy Breaſt their fiery Arrows throw.

Thy

Thy Father, who before the World decreed
His only Son for Human Kind fhou'd bleed,
HisHand withThunder arms,his Brow withDread
To ftrike Thee to the Regions of the Dead :
My God, My God, aloud the Saviour cries,
Why haft forfaken me *?* then bows his Head and
    dies.

His Paffion Univerfal Nature moves,
Except ungrateful Sinners whom he loves,
The trembling Earth her Maker's Sufferings feels,
Her Pillars fhake, her low Foundation reels ;
The Rocks are torn by his expiring Groans ;
The rending Vale his facred Priefthood owns :
The Sun afham'd withdraws his fickly Light,
And turns bright Noon into fubftantial Night,
Afraid to view thofe gafhly Wounds agen.
Nothing relentlefs but the Hearts of Men !

Dear LORD, I in thy Crofs fuch Wonders fee,
Nothing befides has any Charms for me ;
         b   Beneath

Beneath thy Crofs, O may I ftill refide ;

View and review thy Feet, thy Hands, thy
  Head, thy Side !

O how thy Sighs do from my Heart rebound !

And all thy dying Pangs my Bofom wound !

Nor is it Pity only makes me weep ;

No fingle Paffion ftrikes the Heart fo deep :

Hatred of Sin, and Love of Thee combine,

With holy Rage repenting Sorrows join

To make thy Torments intimately mine.

Since 'twas my Sin for which my Saviour dy'd,

'Tis juft I fhould with him be crucify'd :

My Sins procur'd the Crofs, the Whip, the Steel,

Made Thee unutterable Tortures feel :

My Sins ! O that they never had been mine !

I hate them as my Enemys and thine :

My Sins ! O how their Horror makes me ftart,

While I behold their Stains, and feel their Smart,

And fee 'em pierce thy Limbs, and break thy
  Heart !

(flide,

But fince the Balm, that from thy Wounds did

Could heal a Sinner dying at thy Side ;

Thy

Thy Smiles could calm frail *Peter*'s guilty Fears,

And thy Blood cleanse the Stain that he had
　soak'd in Tears :

Since thou haft born th'unfufferable Weight

Of a World's Sins, both Numberlefs and Great ;

LORD, hear a Penitent that proftrate lies,

And at thy feet for pard'ning Mercy cries;

To be reveng'd on Sin implores thy Aid,

Bathing with Tears thy Wounds, the Wounds
　his Sins have made.

O let thy Hands that bled, their Balm apply !

Tho Sin cries loud, thy Blood does louder cry ;

Thy Smiles will make me live, thy Frowns
　will make me die.

But if I die, I'll perifh at thy feet,

And waiting at thy Crofs my Sentence meet.

Sure He, who dy'd for Sinners, won't defpife

A Sinner's broken Heart and flowing Eyes.

O LORD, refolve my Doubts, difpel my Fears,

Supprefs my Sighs, and wipe away my Tears;

Or while thy Charms my wondring Thoughts
　employ,

Turn Floods of Sorrow into Tears of Joy.

　　　　　　　　　{Tis

'Tis done—Thy Groans and Cries thy Love
  refound,
Writ with thy Blood, ingrav'd in ev'ry Wonnd :
The Torture of thy Crofs my Pain allays,
Changing my mournful Sighs to Hymns of Praife.

O JESUS! how Divinely fair Thou art!
Thy Charms have reach'd the Center of my Heart,
Thy Graces all excite refin'd Defire,
How pure the Flame fed by Celeftial Fire!
Strong are the Bands that Hearts in Friendfhip join,
But ftronger Ties have link'd my Soul to Thine.
Had I ten thoufand Hearts, thofe Hearts fhould be
A voluntary Sacrifice to Thee,
To Thee, whofe every Scar fo fully proves
Thy Flame exceeds ten thoufand other Loves.
O'ercome with Love and Wonder, I refign
My Captive Heart, which now no more is mine :
I yield my Soul to thy Victorious Charms,
And fly for Grace to thy inviting Arms :
Life will be Death, if I'm exil'd from Thee ;
Death will be Life, if I thy Face may fee.
                        Thy

Thy Loveliness is equal to thy Love,
And far out-shines Angelick Forms above
LORD, if thy Cross could ne'er thy Beauties hide,
How dost Thou shine at thy Great Father's Side!
Where the Ambitious Flames of Glory now
With emulous Beams salute thy lightning Brow;
Pointing, as in bright Crouds they dart around
Where each rude Thorn thy Sacred Head did
     wound.

While others Thee and their own Souls abuse,
Debase their Love, and prostitute their Muse;
O Thou to whom all Love and Praise belongs!
To Thee I give my Heart, to Thee my Songs.
Waters will rise as high as whence they flow;
So Minds, that came from Heaven, to Heaven
     should go,
With holy Fervor to their Author move,
Who gave 'em Pow'r to think and Pow'r to love.

Eternal Beauty! I thy Rays admire,
Kindling my Flame at that immortal Fire,
                 Where

Where shining *Seraphs* light and cherish theirs;
Thou shalt my Praises have, and thou my Prayers.

May all harmonious Souls their Numbers join,
And each a pious Offering add to mine ;
Make Earth below resemble Heav'n above,
Sing Holy Songs, and sing of Holy Love.
'Tis Love *does with eternal Joys inspire*
All the bright Orders of the Heav'nly Choir :
Seraphick Psalmists to this Noble Theme
Owe their sweet Musick and Poetick Flame.
O may the listning Saints on Earth aspire
To reach the Sound, *and catch the holy Fire !*
And in their turn with pure Devotion sing
The Praises of their Saviour and their King ;
Till Eccho thro Heav'n's Arches loud repeats
The Sound, inviting Angels from their Seats
To hear the *Musick* of the Church below,
While this from t'other Heav'n they scarce can
  know :
Nor an Eclipse of Light and Pleasure fear,
Where they so much of *Grace,* so much of
  Glory hear.

J. S.

A
TABLE
To find any HYMN, if one
knows its Beginning.

Let

The

The more difficult Words explain'd.

Antitype, —— { that which is represented by a Type or Figure.

aſſume, —— receive.

attract, —— draw.

commemorate, bring to remembrance.

deplore, —— bewail.

Effuſion, —— pouring forth.

exil'd, —— baniſh'd.

expiate, —— make Satisfaction for.

extinguiſh, — quench.

Hero, —— a Man of a Noble Spirit.

imbibe, —— drink up.

infernal, —— helliſh.

myſtick, —— ſecret, or obſcure.

Odor, —— ſweet Smell.

proſtrate, —— with the Face to the Ground.

revere, —— reſpect or reverence.

ſatiate, —— ſatisfy.

vital, —— living.

Victim, —— ſacrifice.

Symbol, —— a Sign.

HYMNS

Sacramental Hymns,

BOOKS *written by the same Author.*

A Version of *Solomon's Song of Songs,* fit to be bound with these Hymns.

Advice to the Young, or the Reasonableness and Advantages of an early Conversion, in 3 Sermons on *Ecclef* 1°. 1. To which is added a Funeral Discourse on *2 Cor* 5. 4. The second Edition.

A Poem to the Memory of the late King *William* III. of Glorious Memory. The third Edition.

A Thanksgiving Sermon for the late Glorious Victory obtain'd over the *French* and *Bavarians* at *Blenheim* near *Hochstet.*

A Thanksgiving Sermon, preach'd *Jun* 26. 1706. on occasion of the Battel at *Ramilly,* and raising the Siege of *Barcelona.*

A Thanksgiving Sermon, preach'd *May* 1 1707. for the Happy Union of *England* and *Scotland.*

An Answer to Mr. *Russen's* Book, intitled, *Fundamentals without a Foundation,* a true Picture of the *Anabaptists,* &c

All sold by *J Baker* at *Mercers Chap* in *Cheapside.*

HYMNS
FOR THE
Lord's Supper.

HYMN I.

JEHOVAH, we in Hymns of Praise
    Thy matchlefs Grace adore,
That Grace that gave thy only Son,   *Rom* 8.32.
    What couldft thou give us more?

He's *All in All*, his Saints in Him   *Col.* 3. 11.
    Divine Perfection view;   *Eph.* 1. 23.
'Tis of his Fulnefs they receive   *John* 1.16.
    All *Grace*, and *Glory* too.   *Pf.* 84 11.

He freely gave his Blood, the Price   1 *Pet.* 1.
    Of our Eternal Blifs :   18, 19.
Since no lefs could atone for Sin,   *Heb.* 9.22,
    His Love would give no lefs.   23.

He in the Wine-prefs of thy Wrath   *Lam.*1.15.
    For guilty Men was crufht;
Humbled himfelf to die, and laid   *Phil.* 2. 8
    His Honour in the Duft.

B   That

That we might at his *Table* fit,
    And be replenifh'd there
1 *Cor.* 11. With thefe Dear Pledges of his *Grace*,
26.   Till we his *Glory* fhare.

H Y M N II.

1 *John* 4.
8, 16.   THOU art *All Love*, my deareft LORD,
*Cant.*5.16.   Thou art *All Lovely* too :
        Thy Love I at thy Table taft,
Pfal. 27.4.   Thy Lovelinefs I view.

*Ifa.*53.2,3. Thy Divine Beauty, vail'd with Flefh,
        Thy Enemys defpife ;
        Thy mangled Body they difdain,
        And turn from Thee their Eyes.

Cant. 5. 9, But thou *more* Lovely art to me
&c.   For all that thou haft born ;
John 13.   Each Cloud fets off thy Luftre more,
31, 32.   Thee all thy Scars adorn.

*Ifa.*63.1,2. Thy Garments tinctur'd with thy Blood,
        The beft and nobleft Dye,
Pfal. 45.2. Out-fhine the Robes that Princes wear ;
        Thy Thorns their Gems out-vie.

Pf. 73.25. That I may be *All Love* to Thee,
Cant. 1.   And *Lovely* like Thee too,
15, 16.   O cleanfe me with thy precious Blood,
*Zech.*13 1. And me thy Beauty fhew.
2 *Cor.*3.18.

                    My

My former Vows I now renew :   *Pfal.* 119.
  O LORD, as Thou art Mine ;   106.
I freely give my Heart to Thee,   *Cant.*2.16.
  For ever I'll be Thine.

H Y M N III.

[*As the* 100 *Pfalm.*]

THat doleful Night, when our dear LORD *Joh.* 18.1.
  Into the Garden did retreat,
To vent his Grief in Groans, and Cries, *Luk.*22.44
In Tears, and in a bloody Sweat ;

That ne'er to be forgotten Night,
When our Redeemer was betray'd ;   1 *Cor.* 11.
Before his Sufferings he took Bread,   23,24,25.
Gave Thanks to God, broke it, and faid,

Take, eat, this is my Body broke
For you upon the Curfed Tree :   *Mat.* 26.
Perform this Ord'nance as I do,   26,27,28.
And when you do't, remember Me.

He took the Cup too, crown'd with Wine,
Blefs'd it, and to's Difciples faid,
'Tis the New Teft'ment in my Blood,
For you, and many others fhed.

All you, my Friends, muft drink of this,
Your Sin's Remiffion here you fee ;
Perform this Ord'nance as I do,
And when you do't, remember Me.

Cant. 1. 4. Yes, LORD, we will remember Thee,
       And thy Love more than fragrant Wine :
Rev. 5. 9, How can we e'er thy Cross forget,
10.   Which made Thee ours, and made us Thine?

Pfal. 137. Our right Hand first shall lose its Art,
5, 6.   Our Tongues forget to speak or move,
       E'er we'l prove thoughtless of thy Wounds,
       Those Everlasting Marks of Love.

1 Cor. 11. We'll thus commemorate thy Death,
26.   Till thou appear on Earth again:
       And, LORD, remember us, we pray;
Rev. 11. Make haste to take thy Power, and reign.
17.

H Y M N IV.

Pfal. 24. 7. Behold the *King of Glory* sits
Cant. 1. 12.   At Table with his Guests :
       Welcomes them all with gracious Smiles,
       Them all with Dainties feasts.

       No common Food he here presents,
John 6.   No common Drink provides :
50—58. For Meat he gives his Flesh ; for Wine
Joh. 19. 34.   The Spear his Heart divides.

1 Cor. 11. LORD, give us Faith to raise our Thoughts
28, 29.   Beyond the views of Sense :
       Teach us thy Myst'ries to discern,
       And draw new Joys from thence.

                                Let's

Let's know thy wounded Body fell   *Ifa.*53.5,6.
    An Offering for our Guilt;
Let's know, to wafh us from our Sins,
    Thy Heart's pure Blood was fpilt.

So fhall our Minds and Voices join   1 *Cor.* 14.
    In facred Harmony,   15.
To celebrate thy Grace, and fing
    Hallelujah to Thee.

H Y M N V.

TO us our God his Love commends,   *Rom.* 5. 8.
    When by our Sins undone;
That he might fpare his Enemies,
    He wou'd not fpare his Son,   *Rom.*8 32.

His only Son, on whom he plac'd   *Prov* 8.
    All his Delight and Love,   22—30.
Before he form'd the Earth below,
    Or fpread the Heavens above.

He chaig'd the Darling of his Soul   *John* 3.
    To veil his Glorious Face,   16, 17.
To wear our mortal Flefh, and feel
    The Pains of Human Race,

Our Sorrows and our Sins to bear,
    Our heavy Crofs fuftain;   *Gal.* 3. 13,
Upon a Tree to bleed and die,   14.
    That we might Life obtain:

    This

Col. 3. 3, 4. This Life is hid in God with Him,
           Who fell a Sacrifice,
Heb. 2. 14. And Dying conquer'd Death for us,
Phil. 3. 21.   That we like Him might rise .

Acts 2. 24. For he soon triumph'd o'er the Grave,
Acts 1. 9.   And went to Heaven again ;
   ver. 11. There intercedes, and thence will come
Rev. 20. 4.   Among his Saints to reign.

Heb 10 37 His Word assures he'l quickly come,
Rom. 8.   Saints for his Coming pray,
19——22. The whole Creation for it groans,
Rev. 22.   LORD Jesus, *come away.*
20.

H Y M N VI.

[*As the* 100 *Psalm.*]

Joh. 14. 18. DEscend, O King of Saints, descend :
Ps. 51. 12.   By thy free Spirit's vital Heat
Fresh Joys to every Soul extend,
That at thy Table finds a Seat.

     O Prince of Peace, bless thou this Board
Mat. 18. With those sweetSmileswhichAngels chear;
10   O give us Peace ; and tell us, LORD,
Luke 7. We're pardon'd, and accepted here.
47, 48.

     As thou our hungry Souls hast fed,
Mat. 5. 6. Our thirsty Souls sustain'd with Wine ;
John 6   Nourish us with this heav'nly Bread,
55, 56. And with this Sacred Blood of thine.

Teach

Teach us to wash our Garments clean   *Rev.* 7.14.
In the pure Fountain of thy Blood;   *Zech.* 13.1.
LORD, purge our Souls from every Stain
I'tn' Streams of that All-cleansing Flood.

Each Sin of ours has been a Thorn,   *Isa.* 53.4,
A cruel Nail, a Whip, a Spear;   5, 6.
By these thy sacred Flesh was torn,
These did thy Soul with Horror tear.

Yet every Wound of thine does yield   *Luk.* 10 34
A Balsam for a contrite Heart,
Which, on the painful Sore distil'd,
Heals and allays the tort'ring Smart.

Amazing Love! 'Tis Infinite!   *Eph.* 3.18,
No Thoughts its endless Depth can sound;   19.
It Heaven's high Arch exceeds for height, *Ps.* 108.4.
And for Extent, the World's vast Round.

LORD, to advance thy Praises here,   *Ps.* 51. 15,
Increase our Light, inlarge our Love;
And by thy Grace our Souls prepare   *Rev.* 5. 9.
For better Songs and Tunes above.

H Y M N VII.

(share,
YOU who our LORD's great Banquet
    And welcome Places find   *Mat.* 26.
His Table round, his Praises sound   30.
    With well-tun'd Voice and Mind.

Remember all his Acts of Love,
 His Torments every one :
Heb. 1. 6. Whom Angels fear'd, him Mortals jeer'd,
Mat. 27. Blasphem'd and spat upon.
30.

 Ver 29. See's Head all torn with Thorns, his Face
Cant. 5.10, (Divinely bright before)
16. Now mar'd more than the Sons of Men,
Isa. 52.14. Reaking with Sweat and Gore.

Ps. 22.16. See in his Hands and Feet the Nails
  Piercing the tender Veins :
 See how each Wound the blushing Ground
  With precious Tincture stains.

Joh. 19.34 See his Side spout a stream of Blood
  And Water thro the Wound ;
1 *John* 1.7. A Stream wherein we're wash'd from Sin,
  And all our Guilt is drown'd.

 But, Oh! what Terrors wrack'd his Soul
  In that last Agony,
Mat. 27. When (e'er he dy'd) *My God,* he cry'd,
46. *Why hast forsaken me !*

Joh. 10. Thus groan'd and dy'd the Son of God,]
10, 11. That we might ever live
1 *Cor.* 2. 9. There, where all Bliss our Souls can wish,
  Or can contain, He'll give.

 Mean while the Myst'ries of his Grace
1 *Cor.* 11. His Table here displays ;
26. O how his Love our Souls should move,
  And Tongues to sing his Praise!

       H Y M N

H Y M N   VIII.

MY Soul, let all thy nobler Powers,   *Pf.*104. 1.
  And Faculties combine :
Awake my Tongue, and to my Thoughts *Pf.* 57 8.
  Thy tuneful Numbers join.

All that's within me, blefs and praife   *Pfal.* 103.
  My Saviour and my King.   1, 2
When he's the Subject of the Song,   *Rev.* 15.
  Who can forbear to fing?   3, 4.

Holy and Reverend is his Name ;   *Pf.*111. 9.
  How glorious, and how fweet
All Greatnefs, and all Goodnefs too
  I' th' Name of JESUS meet:

                                            *Rev.*6.15,
A Name vile Men fhall one day dread,   16, 17.
  As now the Devils fear .   *Jam.*2.19.
A Name the Heavenly Hofts adore,   *Mat* 8.29.
  To pardon'd Sinners dear ;   *Rev.*5.11,
                                             12.
Moft dear to them by ftrongeft Ties   *Cant.*1. 3.
  Of his Redeeming Love,
Which by a thoufand Torments try'd,
  Did ever conftant prove.

Tho Death and Hell unite their Powers
  T' oppofe his Enterprize,
The fpotlefs Lamb refolves to fall   *Joh.*10.11
  A willing Sacrifice.

                                    So

*Heb.*2.14.   So conquering Sin, and Death, and Hell,
                 In Glory did arise,
Acts 1. 9.   And in bright Triumph soon ascend
                 His Throne above the Skies.

Jude 14.   Thence in due time he will return,
1 *Thess.*4.   With a Celestial Train,
16, 17.   Of Saints and Angels, who shall sing
                 The Wonders of his Reign.

H Y M N   IX.

*Heb.*10.19
*Psal.*2.11   WIth humble Boldness, trembling Joy,
*Heb.*12 28   With Hope and awful Fear,
               LORD, we thy Majesty address,
Ver. 22.   And to thy Seat draw near.

Gen 18.25   For Thou, Great Judg of all the Earth,
Heb. 4 16.   Now on a Throne of Grace,
*Psal.*80 1.   Between the wondring *Cherubs* Wings
                   Reveal'st thy glorious Face.

Rom 8.34.   At thy right Hand behold thy Son,
                   Who kindly intercedes:
*Heb.*12.24   His Blood crys louder than our Sins,
                   And for our Pardon pleads.

Isa. 53. 5. Ah cruel Sins, how odious now,
                   And how deform'd are they,
Deu 9. 26.   While in that Crimson Fountain we
                   Their monstrous Hue survey

                                    These

These with black Horror fill'd his Mind, *Mat.* 26.
    Inrag'd his Wounds with Pain   38.
These rent with Grief his laboring Breast, *Pf.* 22. 14.
    Exhausted every Vein.

Tho these our Crimes all testify   *Jer.* 14. 7.
    Our crying Guilt aloud;   *Gen.* 18. 21.
LORD, vail no more thy shining Face   *Lam.* 3. 44.
    Within an angry Cloud.

Let thy Love's Rays attract from us
    A Penitential Dew;   *Luke* 7.
And while our Vileness we lament,   38, 47.
    Thy pard'ning Mercy shew:

Then tho our Sins have numerous been   *Pf.* 40. 12.
    Like Sands upon the shore;
Peace like a River flouds our Souls,   *Isa.* 48. 18.
    And Sins are seen no more.

HYMN X.

[*As the* 100 *Psalm.*]

IN grateful Hymns, ye Saints, display *Eph.* 3. 18,
  JEHOVAH's Grace and boundless Love;   19.
A Love, whose Flame inspires the Songs *Rev.* 5. 9.
Of all the Heav'nly Host above.

Tho we on Earth can't sing like them,   *Pfal.* 103.
Let's praise him in a lower strain: 20, 21, 22.
A fervent Mind, that breathes his Praise 1 *Sam.* 16.
With stammering Lips, He'l not disdain. 7.

                                Eter-

Eternal Father, we adore
*Ifa.*53.10. Thy Love, that mov'd Thee to expofe
The facred Body of thy Son
To bear the Wounds due to thy Foes.

1 *Cor.* 15. And Thee, dear Saviour, we adore,
56.   Who didft endure th' invenom'd Sting
*Gal.*3.13. Of Death, and every dreadful Curfe
Juftice provok'd by Sin could bring.

While we behold Thee on thy Crofs,
In every Wound thy Love appears,
Pf. 63. 3. Dearer than Life, more ftrong than Death,
*Cant.*8. 6 Flowing in Streams of Blood and Tears.

*Zech.*13.1 To bathe our Souls defil'd by Sin,
LORD, we approach this Sacred Flood;
To heal our broken Hearts, we feek
Luk 10.34 The Sovereign Balfam of thy Blood.

Ifa. 55. 1. 'Tis from this Living Stream our Souls,
Our dying Souls new Life derive;
*Pfal.*23.5. This is the Sacred Oil of Joy,
That can defponding Minds revive.

*Pfal.*24.7. O King of Glory, on us fhine,
Who thy own Table now furround;
Ifa. 59. 2. Let not our Sins eclipfe thy Face,
Job 33.24 Since thou haft fuch a Ranfom found.

H Y M N

H y m n XI.

[*As the* 25 *Pſalm.*]

IMmortal Praiſe be given,   *Luk.*2.14.
   And Glory in the high'ſt,
To th'God of Peace,who ſent from Heaven
   His own beloved Chriſt ;   *Pſal.* 2.2.

Him a Sin-Offering made   *Iſa.* 53.10.
   For *Adam*'s Guilty Sons ;
Our preſſing Crimes upon him laid,   *Ver.* 6.
   For which his Blood atones.   *Heb.* 9 14.

Such Torments He endur'd   *Pſal.*22. 1,
   As none e'er felt before,   6,14,15--.
That Joy and Bliſs might be ſecur'd   *Iſa.*53-3,4-
   To us for evermore.

                         Luke 23.
Hurry'd from Bar to Bar,   7, 11. &
   With Blows and Scoffs abus'd ; 22. 63,64.
Revil'd by *Herod*'s Men of War,   *Luk.*23.11.
   With *Pilate*'s Scourges bruis'd. *Mat.* 27.
                          26.

His ſweet and Reverend Face
   With Spittle all profan'd ;   *Mat.* 27.
That Viſage, full of Heav'nly Grace, 29, 30.
   With his own Blood diſtain'd.

Stretch'd on the cruel Tree,   *Mat.* 27.
   He bled, and groan'd, and cry'd ; 46, 50.
And in a mortal Agony
   Languiſh'd awhile, and dy'd.

                               But

Heb. 2.14.   But dying left a Wound
Gen. 3 15.   On the Old Serpent's Head,
            For which no Cure can e'er be found ;
Mat. 28.   And soon rose from the Dead :
1, 6.
Acts 1. 9,   Then did to Heaven ascend,
10.   That we might thither go,
Joh 14. 2   Where Love and Praises have no end,
*1Cor.*13.8   Where Joys no Changes know.
*Rev.*21 4.

H Y M N XII.

GRacious Redeemer, how Divine,
        How wondrous is thy Love !
Rev. 5.   The Subject of th' Eternal Songs
9———14   Of Blessed Spirits above.

            Join in the sacred Harmony,
Isa. 7. 14.   Ye Saints on Earth below,
*Mat.*1.23. To praise *Immanuel*, from whose Name
Cant. 1. 3.   All fragrant Odors flow.

*Phil.*2.6,7 He left his Crown, he left his Throne
            By his Great Father's side ,
        Wore Thorns, sustain'd a heavy Cross,
        Was scourg'd and crucify'd.

*Gal.*3. 13, His was the Torment, his the Curse ;
14.   Tho all the Guilt was ours :
Lev. 14.   To cleanse us, on our Leprous Souls
            His Vital Blood he pours.

                                Be

Behold how every Wound of his
  A precious Balm diſtils,   *Luke* 10.
Which heals the Scars that Sin had made, 34.
  With Joy the Sinner fills.

                (Grace ;
Thoſe Wounds are Mouths that preach his *Joh.*12.32.
  The Characters of Love ;   *Gal.* 3. 1.
The Seals of our expected Bliſs   *Rom.*8. 32.
  In Paradiſe above.

We ſee thee at thy Table, *LORD*,
  By Faith, with great delight :
O how refin'd thoſe Joys will be   *2 Cor.* 5.7.
  When Faith is turn'd to Sight !

H y m n XIII.

THE God of Grace to Human Race   *Rom.* 5. 8.
  Does Terms of Peace propoſe ,
He gives his Son, his only One,
  A Ranſom for his Foes.   *Rom.* 5.10.

Chriſt to fulfil his Father's Will,   *John* 10.
  Himſelf as freely gave,   11, 15.
An Offering whole, Body and Soul,   1 *Pet.* 2.
  A guilty World to ſave.   24.
                       Iſa. 53.10.

The Spirit Divine, for this Deſign,
  Lights on him like a Dove :   *Mat.* 3.16.
The Sacred Three in One agree,   1 *John* 5.
  In this great Act of Love.   7.

                    Juſtice

Pf. 85. 10. Juftice and Grace like Friends embrace,
        With equal Splendor fhine ;
        No Gift could be fo Rich, fo Free,
        So Glorious, fo Divine.

        Bleft Saviour, why fhould we deny
          To Thee, at thy Defire,
Rom. 12: An Offering whole, Body and Soul,
1, 2.   As Reafon does require ?

        Since thou for us haft born a Crofs,
1 *John* 4.   Tho free from every Crime ;
19.   How great fhould be our Love to Thee,
Rev. 5. 12. Our Praifes how fublime !

H Y M N XIV.

      [*As the* 100 *Pfalm.*]   (Train
Rom. 6. 23. WHen Sin had brought Death, with a
Rom. 3. 19.   Of Miferies on the guilty World,
        And wretched Man was doom'd to be
2 *Pet.* 2. 17 Into Eternal Darknefs hurl'd ;

Mar. 9. 44, Where the tormenting Worm, that gnaws
46, 48.   The feftering Confcience, ne'er expires;
Rev. 20. Where tort'ring Brimftone always feeds
10, 15.   The ne'er-to-be extinguifh'd Fires:

Gen. 3 24. When Juftice wav'd the flaming Sword
1 *Tim.* 2 5. Of Vengeance o'er the Sinner's Head ;
        The Son of God ftept in, and ftay'd
        The Mortal Stroke, and thus he faid:
                  The

Tho all the Offerings Men can bring	*Pfal.* 40. 6.
Can't for one single Crime atone ;	*Ver* 7.
O God, I come to do thy Will,	*Heb.* 10.
I'll bear their numerous Sins alone.	4——10.

A Mortal Nature I'll affume,	*Heb.* 2. 16.
Human Infirmities I'll wear ;	*Mat.* 4. 2.
Hunger, and Thirſt, and Wearineſs,	*Joh.* 4 6, 7.
Sorrows and Pains I'll freely bear.	*Heb.* 4. 15.

Reproaches, tho they'll break my Heart,	*Pf.* 69. 20.
I am reſolv'd to undergo :	*Iſa.* 53. 10.
I'll ſuffer all that's on me laid	*Pfal.* 22.
By God above, or Men below.	12——18.

Tho all th' Infernal Powers conſpire	*Mat.* 4. 1.
My Great Deſign to overthrow ;	*Luk.* 22. 53.
Thro Showers of fiery Darts from Hell,	*Eph.* 6 16.
And thro Death's horrid Vale I'll go.	*Pfal.* 23. 4.

Thus ſaid, the Father ſoon reply'd :	
Content, I have a Ranſom found ;	*Job* 33. 24.
Dear Son, to ſave a ruin'd World,	
Ev'n Thee I with Delight ſhall wound.	*Iſa.* 53. 10.

Go execute thy brave Reſolves,	
Thy Sufferings ſhall rewarded be ;	*Ver.* 11, 12.
Many Tnou ſhalt redeem, the reſt	
Shall all at laſt be judg'd by Thee.	*Acts* 17. 31

How precious are theſe Thoughts of thine,	*Pfal.* 139.
How glorious, *LORD*, theſe Acts of Love !	17, 18.
For theſe we ſing thy Praiſe below,	
For theſe Thou'rt better prais'd above.	*Rev* 5. 11.
	1.

C HYMN

H Y M N XV.

HOW many Miracles of Love,
Col. 1. 26,   What *Myſteries* of Grace
27.   Has th' Ever-bleſſed *Jeſus* ſhown
            To *Adam*'s ſinful Race !

            That he ſhould humbly condeſcend
Rom. 8. 3.   Our mortal Fleſh to wear ;
Mat.8.17.   Our Sickneſſes, our Sorrows all,
            And numerous Sins to bear !

            Was't not enough, thou Holy ONE,
            To lay aſide thy Crown,
Phil. 2. 7. And, in a Servant's Form, on Earth
            To wander up and down ?

Joh.11.33 Was't not enough with Sighs and Tears
& ver. 35.   Our Miſeries to deplore,
Mat. 11.   To teach us by thy blameleſs Life ?
29, 30.   But wouldſt Thou ſtill do more !

            Whence is this unexampled Love
            To wretched Human kind ?
Ezek. 16.   What to attract thy Heart couldſt Thou
5, 6.   In loathſom Sinners find ?

Iſa 53 4,5. Yet loaded with our Sins and Pains,
Pſal. 23.4.   Thou thro Death's Vale wouldſt go,
Pſ 16. 11. That we made Innocent and Free,
Mat.7.14.   The way of Life might know.

                                    Wor-

Worthy art thou, O *Lamb of God*,   *Rev.* 5.12.
  Among thy *Saints* to reign,
Who to redeem them by thy Blood,
  Waſt once an Offering ſlain.

H Y M N XVI.

HOW ſweet, how charming is thePlace, *Pſ.* 84. 1,2.
    With God's bright Preſence crown'd'
Happy his Children, who his Board   *Pſ.* 128. 3.
  As Olive-Plants ſurround.

Eat of this Feaſt, ſays he, my Friends,   *Cant.* 5. 1.
  Who to my Courts repair;
Come, deareſt Children, freely drink   *Prov.* 9. 5.
  The Wine which I prepare.

LORD, we accept thy bounteous Treat,
  With Wonder, Joy, and Love:
O may we in thy Houſe have Place,   *Pſal.* 27.4.
  And never thence remove'

Here may our Faith ſtill on Thee feed,
  The only Food Divine;   *John* 6.
To Faith thy Fleſh is Meat indeed,   50, &c.
  Thy Blood the Nobleſt Wine:

Thy Blood, that purifying Juice,   1 *Joh.* 1.7.
  To cleanſe our Souls deſign'd;
To heal a Sinner's bleeding Heart,   *Luk.* 10.34
  And chear his drooping Mind.

1 *Cor.* 13. Here we are glad to view thy Love,
12.   Thro Figures, and in part;
           But how much greater Joy will't be
1 *Joh.* 3. 2.   *To see thee as thou art !*

H Y M N XVII.

[*As the* 100 *Psalm.*]

Mic. 6, 6. WHerewith shall I a sinful Worm
           Jehovah's Holy Place draw nigh?
With what Oblations shall I bow
Before the Throne of God most High?

          Shall I Burnt Offerings to him bring,
Ver. 7.   Calves taken from their tender Dams?
          Will God be pleas'd, if I should slay
          A thousand and a thousand Rams?

          Shall I upon his Altar pour
          Rivers of Oil ten thousand times;
          Or my First-born an Offering make,
          To expiate my odious Crimes?

Psal 40. 6. No —— God is so incens'd by Sin,
Ps. 51. 16. Such Offerings all would be in vain;
          Too mean to save the guilty Soul,
          And purge it from so foul a Stain.

          With broken Heart and fervent Cries,
Heb. 6. 18. Dear JESUS, to thy Cross I fly;
          Tho other Refuge fail, on Thee
Heb. 7. 25. My Soul with safety can rely.

                        The

The Blood defcending from thy Wounds,
Becomes both Oil and Wine to ours;   *Luk.*10.34.
No Eafe, till thy kind Hand this Balm
Into the wounded Confcience pours.   *Job* 34.29.

As at thy Table we behold
Thy All-fufficient Sacrifice,
Let's feel the Virtue of thy Blood,   *Ifa.* 53. 5.
Which heals, and chears, and purifies.   *Joh.* 6. 54.
                                           1 *Joh.*1.7.

So while thy Sacred Courts we tread,
To Thee, O God, our Life and Joy,   *Pfal.* 43 4.
We'll bring the Sacrifice of Praife,   *Pf.*116.17.
In Praife our Hearts and Tongues imploy. *Pf* 103.1,

H Y M N   XVIII.

O LORD, how fhall we frame a Song   *Job* 37 19,
    To celebrate thy Fame!   20.
Our higheft Flights are all too low
    To reach thy Loftier Name.

Yet fhould the Objects of thy Love
    Thy Praifes ceafe to fhout,
To cenfure fuch Ingratitude,
    The Stones would foon cry out.   *Luk.*19.40

What was there, LORD, in finful Man   *Pf.*144. 3.
    That could thy Pity move,
To draw him from the Gates of Hell
    With charming Bands of Love!   *Hof.* 11. 4.

A Love, by many Sorrows try'd,
Cant. 8.6,   And many a painful Wound ;   (Death,
7.   Whose Flame could not be quench'd by
             Could by no Floods be drown'd ;

             No not by all those Streams of Blood
John 19.2.   Which on thy Cross did meet,
 Ver. 34. From thy pierc'd Heart, and bleeding Head,
Pf. 22. 16.   And wounded Hands and Feet.

Eph. 3.18. A Love whose Wonders far transcend
Exod. 25.   The reach of Human View ;
19, 20. Whose *Myst'ries* the inquiring Crowd
Eph. 3 10.   Of *Cherubs* look into.
1 *Pet.*1.12.

             O happy Men who taft this Grace,
1 *Pet.*2.3.   Which Angels so admire ;
2*Cor.*4.18. And feel the Shines of that bright Face,
             Which they to see desire '

             But when all *Myftick* Truth shall be
             Plac'd in a clearer Light ,
1 *Cor.* 13. What Joy ' *Chrift* Face to Face to see
12,   With full and endless Sight '

HYMN

HYMN XIX.

SING *Hallelujah* to our King,
   Who nobly entertains   *John* 6.35.
His Friends with Bread of Life, and Wine *ver.*50,&c.
   That flow'd from all his Veins.

His Body pierc'd with numerous Wounds,
   Did as a Victim bleed ;   *John* 6.53.
That we might drink his sacred Blood,
   And on his Flesh might feed.

Wormwood and Gall was once his Meat, *Pf.* 69 21.
   His Cup with Terror fill'd,   *Luk.* 22.42
That we might taft the heav'nly Sweet
   His Royal Banquets yield.

When our Redeemer dy'd, he was
   Both Sacrifice and Prieft :   *Heb.* 9. 26.
And now he lives, he is become   *Luke* 22.
   Th' Inviter, and the Feaft.   19, 20.

We feed on Chrift, and fup with him; *Rev.*3 20.
   At Table he prefides
As Ruler of the Feaft, his fhare   *Cant.*1.12.
   To every Gueft divides.

While he Love's Banner here difplays *Cant.* 2.4.
   O'er our Triumphant Heads,
Sin dies, each Grace revives, and foon *Cant.*1.12.
   Its precious Odor fpreads.

Nor are our Pleasures bounded here,
For he's gone to prepare
John 14 2. Mansions, where Heavenly Manna shall
Rev. 2 17.   Be our Eternal Fare.

H Y M M XX.

[*As the 25 Psalm.*]
Luk 2 14.   **G**lory *to God on high,*
            Good Will to Men below :
If thus the Friendly Angels cry,
    What Joy should Mortals show !

Those Angels free from Sin,
Heb. 9. 14.   No bloody Offering need :
Ver. 22. 'T vas for the guilty Sons of Men
    Our Saviour came to bleed.

Luk 2.13.   Yet the kind Heav'nly Host
            With shouting rend the Sky,
2 *Pet.*2. 4. Glad that the Thrones, their *Fellows* lost,
Heb. 2 16.   Redeem'd *Men* shall supply.

What good, what welcome News !
Luk. 2 10.   What wondrous Love is here !
Rom 5. 8. That God his only Son should bruise,
Isa. 53.10.   So Lovely, and so Dear !

That poor Apostate Man
John 14.   In Heav'n might ever dwell,
2, 3.   Who with wild Fury headlong ran
Mat. 7 13·   The way that leads to Hell !

                                Dear

Dear LORD, with what Surprize
Do we thy Sufferings trace;   (Cries, *Eph.* 3. 18,
And mark thy Wounds, thy Groans, thy 19.
Thy Sorrows, and Difgrace !

For all this haft Thou born   *Ifa.*53.4,5.
To expiate our Guilt :
Thy Flefh to heal our Sores was torn,
Thy Blood to cleanfe us fpilt.

Thy Shame deferves Renown,   *Phil.* 2.
Thy Crofs a Princely Throne ;   8—11.
That Head becomes a Royal Crown, *Heb.* 2. 9.
Which wore a thorny one.   *Mat.* 27.
                                 29.

And one day Thou our King
In Glory wilt appear,   2 *Thef.* 1.
And Troops of Saints and Angels bring 7.
T' attend thy Triumph here.   *Jude* 14.

Glory to God on high,   *Luk.* 2.14.
Good Will to Men below :
If thus the Friendly Angels cry,
What Joy fhould Mortals fhow !

HYMN

H Y M N XXI.

[*As the* 100 *Psalm.*]

Mat. 26. FROM Supper to *Gethsemané*
36.   Away our blessed LORD does hast,
      Thither let's follow him, and see
      How he begins of Death to tast.

Pf. 40.12. He saw of Sins an endless Scroul,
Isa. 1. 18. Millions of Sins of Crimson Red,
Isa. 53. 6. All meeting on his spotless Soul,
      While he stood charg'd in Sinners stead.

2Cor.5 11. He knew the Terrors of the LORD,
Rom.6.23. The Censures of his righteous Law,
Gen. 3. 24. Naked the bright avenging Sword,
      And brandish'd o'er his Head he saw.

Mat 26. Horror and Anguish on him seize,
38.   His Soul's o'erwhelm'd with mortal Fears;
Heb. 5. 7. He groans, and as his Pangs increase,
Luk.22.44 Sweats Drops of Blood, weeps Floods of
                             (Tears.

      But who can tell how much he felt
Gal 3 13. On that Curs'd Tree whereon he dy'd?
Psal. 22. While's Heart like flowing Wax did melt,
14, 15.   His Strength was like a Potsherd dry'd.

      There, as his panting Body hung,
Luk 22 53 The Powers of Darkness all combin'd,
Eph 6 16. Their flaming Arrows at him flung,
Heb. 2. 18. To fill with thousand Wounds his Mind
                           Men,

Men, by whofe cruel Hands he bled,   *Acts* 2 23.
Ungrateful Men, for whom he dy'd,   *Ver.* 39.
As void of Pity as of Dread,   *Mat.* 27.
Blafpheme him, and his Pains deride.   39—43.

His very Friends, like timorous Sheep,   *Mat.* 26.
Are fcatter'd from their Shepherd now: 31.
His Father's Anger wounds him deep,   *Ver.* 56.
Down to the Duft this makes him bow.   *Mat.* 27.
   46.

No Pains, no Coft our God would fpare,   1 *Pet.*1 18.
Revolted Sinners to regain;   *Rev* 7. 9.
That they might Robes of Glory wear,   *Ver.* 14.
And with him in his Kingdom reign.   *Rev.* 5. 10.

Praife him ye Angels round his Throne,
Who us in Thought and Might excel;   *Pf.*103. 20
Praife him, his Servants every one,
Who in thefe lower Regions dwell.   *Pf.* 134.1.

Hymn XXII.

MY Bleffed Saviour, is thy Love   *Ephef.* 3.
  So great, fo full, fo free?   18, 19.
Behold I give my Love, my Heart,   *Cant.* 6. 3.
  My Life, my All, to Thee.

I love Thee for the glorious Worth   *Cant.* 5.
  In thy Great Self I fee: 9, &c.
I love Thee for that fhameful Crofs   1 *John* 4.
  Thou haft endur'd for me.   19.

Joh.15.13. No Man of greater Love can boaſt
      Than for his *Friend* to die:
Rom 5.10 But for thy *Enemies* thou waſt ſlain ;
      What Love with thine can vie !

Phil. 2 6. Tho in the very Form of God,
Heb 1. 3.   With Heavenly Glory crown'd,
John 1 14. Thou wouldſt partake of Human Fleſh,
Heb 1 15.   Beſet with Troubles round.

Rom. 8. 3. Thou wouldſt like wretched Man be made
Heb 4. 15.   In every thing but Sin ;
2Pet. 1 4. That we as *like* Thee might become,
      As we *unlike* have been :

Phil. 2.5. Like Thee in Faith, in Meekneſs, Love,
2 Cor.3.18.   In every beauteous Grace ;
      From Glory thus to Glory chang'd,
      As we behold thy Face.

Cant. 1.   O LORD, I'll treaſure in my Soul
3, 4.   The Mem'ry of thy Love:
      And thy Dear Name ſhall ſtill to me
      A grateful Odor prove.

Pſal. 16.3. Thy Friends, *the Excellent on Earth,*
      Shall be my chief delight :
Pſal. 1. 2. And when alone, I'll make thy Law
Pſ.119.97.   My Study Day and Night.

Pſal.84 1. Where Thou doſt pitch thy Tent, and where
Pſal.26.8.   Thy Honour deigns to dwell,
Pſal 29.9. There I'll fix mine, and there reſide,
      There thy Love's Wonders tell.

                                   The

The Pledges of thy Love ſhall there   *Cant.* 2. 5.
   Revive this Heart of mine;   *Cant.* 1. 2.
Thy Love, more fragrant and more ſweet
   Than Bowls of Generous Wine.

H Y M N XXIII.

[*As the* 100 *Pſalm.*]

OUR LORD a Banquet has prepar'd, *Iſa.* 55. 1, 2.
  And every hungry Soul invites;
Among his Friends at Table ſits,   *Cant* 1 12.
To bleſs 'em with refin'd Delights.

The Grape's pure Blood, and Flower of *Deut.* 32.
Are proper Symbols to deſcribe   (Wheat 14.
The Heavenly Bread Believers eat,   *John* 6.
The Sacred Wine which they imbibe.   53—58.

Salem's Great Prince, *Melchiſedeck*,
Prieſt of an Order moſt Divine,   *Gen.* 14 18.
The conquering Patriarch met, and fed   *Pſ.* 110 4
His weary Troops with Bread and Wine.

Of the ſame Order Chriſt our Prieſt,   *Heb* 5. 10.
The other's Antitype, and Lord,   *Ch.* 6. 20.
For Bread his broken Body gives,
And does for Wine his Blood afford.

JESUS the King of Righteouſneſs,   *Heb.* 7. 1, 2.
And Prince of Peace, to entertain
Victorious Saints who bear his Arms,   *Rom.* 8 37.
Was willing to be bruis'd and ſlain.   *John* 6 52.

               From

Col. 3. 4.   *From* Thee alone, O LORD of Life,
John 6.   Our Souls their Life of Grace derive :
32, 33.   *By* Thee, the true and living Bread,
Gal. 2. 20. We're daily fed and kept alive.

2 *Cor.* 5.   To Thee, LORD, we resolve to live,
15.   To thee who dost our Life sustain ;
1 *Theſſ.* 4   And with Thee hope to live at laſt,
16, 17.   With Thee eternally to reign.

H Y M N XXIV.

Pſal. 96. 1.   A Ngels and Men, your Songs renew,
            Sing All with pious Mirth ;
Pſ. 96. 11. Rejoice and ſhout, ye Heavens above,
          And be thou glad, O Earth.

Rom. 8. 3. His Son the GOD of Grace ſent down
         With ſinful Men to dwell,
John 8.   The wretched Captives to redeem
24, 36.   From the wide Jaws of Hell.

Heb. 9.   So heinous were our Crimes, ſo great
9——12.   Our Guilt, that nothing leſs
1 *Pet* 1.   Than the Effuſion of his Blood
18, 19   Could purchaſe our Releaſe.
Heb. 10 19
1 *Theſſ.* 1. His Blood his Father's Wrath atones,
10   Quenches Infernal Fire,
1 *Cor* 15. Diſarms Death of its poiſon'd Sting,
55, 56, 57.   Makes Hell's black Troops retire.
Heb. 2. 14.

                                  F

He gain'd this Victory alone,   *Ifa.* 63. 3.
  We in the Triumph fhare ;
He wore our Thorns, that we with Him   *Rev.* 7. 9.
  Might Crowns of Glory wear.   & 2. 10.

Thy Love, **O LORD** *our Righteoufhefs*,   *Jer.* 23. 6.
  Our higheft Thoughts tranfcends ;   *Eph.* 2. 18.
Divinely Free, and knows no Bounds ;   *Pfal.* 136.
  Conftant, and never ends.   1, &c.

O may that Joy thy Favor brings,   *Phil.* 4. 7.
  In all our Souls abound !
So while our King at Table fits,   *Cant.*5.12.
  Our Tongues his Praife fhall found.   *Ver.* 4.

Of the fweet Fruits of Paradife,   *Ephef.* 1.
  Thou giv'ft us here a Taft ;   13, 14.
Wifely referving for thy Friends
  The beft Wine to the laft,   *John* 2. 10.

To that bright endlefs Day, when we
  Shall hidden Manna eat   *Rev.* 2. 17.
Amid the Heav'nly *Eden*, where   *Ver.* 7.
  Our Blifs fhall be compleat.

H Y M N

H Y M N XXV.

Pfal. 8.   LORD, all the Works thy Hand has form'd
           In Earth and Heaven above,
Pf. 107. 8, And all thy Tracks of Providence
15, 21, 31. Shew Thee a God of *Love.*

1 *John* 4. But thy furprizing Acts of Grace
10.   To *Adam's* guilty Seed,
        Loudly proclaim to all the World,
& 4. 8, 16. That *God is* LOVE indeed.

        To Objects who deferve thy **Wrath**
Rom. 5.   Thy boundlefs *Love* extends ;
8, 10.   Thou'rt kinder to thy Enemies
Joh. 15 13. Than Men are to their Friends.

Eph. 1. 4, *Love* drew the Model of our Blifs
5, 6, 7.   In the Decrees Divine ;
        Conducts the Work, and will at length
John 13.1. Compleat the vaft Defign.

        Love brought Heav'n's Heir down from his
Mat. 1. 23. Into a Virgin's Womb,   (Throne
        Faften'd him to a Curfed Tree,
Joh. 19.41. And laid him in a Tomb.

        In his Words, Deeds, and Sufferings all,
Prov. 31.   The Law of Kindnefs reign'd ;
26.   *Love* open'd all his ghaftly Wounds,
1 *John* 4. Thro which his Life was drain'd.
10.

                               His

His *Love* as freely tenders now
  That meritorious Blood,   *John* 6.
That broken Body, to our Souls   51, &c.
  The beſt and ſweeteſt Food.

Love carry'd him up to his Throne,   *Joh.*16.17.
  There to prepare us room ;
And *Love* will bring him down again   *Heb.* 9.28.
  At laſt, to lead us home.   1 *Theſſ.* 4.
                             17.

H Y M N XXVI.

[*As the* 100 *Pſalm.*]
HAſt Thou, my Soul, thy Saviour view'd *Acts* 5. 30.
  As on the Croſs he hung and bled?
Haſt ſeen his Bruiſes, Wounds, and Tears, *Heb.* 5.7,8.
Seen him bow down his dying Head ?

Haſt heard how rudely he was jeer'd   *Mat.* 27.
By thoſe that made him groan and die ? 39—43.
Heard him amid their cruel Scoffs,
Ev'n rend the Heavens with his Cry,   *Mat.* 27.
                                46.
That doleful Cry, *My God, my God,*   Ver. 50.
O why haſt thou thy Son forſook !
Haſt mark'd the Anguiſh of his Words,
The mortal Horror of his Look ?

All this is much, yet 'tis not All ;
But thou no proper Terms canſt find   *Iſa.*53. 10.
To paint the Torments of his Soul,
The inward Bruiſes of his Mind.
         · D   All

All this and more than thou, my Soul,
Isa. 53. 6. Canst tell or think, he did endure,
To skreen thee from his Father's Wrath,
And thy Eternal Bliss secure.

Look back once more, and view his Head,
Isa. 52. 14. His Back, his Hands, his Feet, his Side,
And tell if any Sight like this
Is found in all the World beside.

Phil. 3. 8. No, all to me is Dung and Dross,
But my dear JESUS crucify'd:
Gal. 2. 3. Under the Shadow of his Cross
I'll sit me down, and there abide.

Joh. 15. 13 His Wounds, the noblest Proofs of Love,
Cant. 5. 16. His Beauty too I there shall see,
Ezek. 16. Darting thro his reproachful Veil
14.   Its sweet and powerful Beams on me.

HYMN XXVII.

[As the 25 Psalm.]

Psal. 2. 16. LORD, we approach thy Throne,
Psb. 13. 15   To thee Thank-Offerings bring;
Psal. 29. 9. For in thy Temple every one
             Should of thy Glory sing.

Ps. 68. 16.   There Thou art pleas'd to dwell,
Ps. 27. 4.   And there thy Beauty shines;
             There to thy Fav'rites Thou dost tell
Ps. 25. 14.   Thy great, thy good Designs.

                                    Thy

Thy Table they draw near,   *Cant.* 5. 1.
  To which thy Calls invite,
They find the beſt of Dainties there,
  And There to dwell delight.

Thy Fleſh is Meat indeed,   *Joh* 6. 55.
  Thy Blood the richeſt Wine;
How bleſt are they who often feed
  On this Repaſt of thine!

While by our Sins to Thee   *Mat.* 26.
  We fill'd a bitter Cup,   39.
Thou mad'ſt this Noble Treat, that we   & 27. 34.
  Might at thy Table ſup.   & 26 26

May Joy, with humble Fear,   *Pſal.* 2. 11.
  A true Devotion raiſe
In all who are aſſembled here,
  To celebrate thy Praiſe.

So while thy Courts reſound
  With Songs, we ſhall confeſs
That no ſuch Pleaſure's to be found   *Pſ* 84. 10
  I' th' Tents of Wickedneſs.

And if ſuch Feaſts as this   *Pſal.* 36.
  Yield ſo much Sweet below,   7, 8.
What Joys ſwim in thoſe Floods of Bliſs,   *Pſ.* 16. 11.
  Which at thy right Hand flow?

Hymn

H Y M N XXVIII.

Ps. 51. 17. O LORD, Thou do∫t a broken Heart
And contrite Mind approve,
Wilt humble Penitents receive
With Pity, Joy, and Love.

Psal. 2. 11. Teach us o'er all our Sins to weep,
And in thy Grace rejoice ;
Pf. 130. 4. To mix Confessions of our Guilt
With a Thanksgiving Voice.

Jn 16. 8, O let thy Spirit's Convincing Power
9, 10, 11. Dispose us to repent,
1 Th 2. 2c. That Holy Oil will soften Rocks,
Acts 2. 37. Make flinty Hearts relent.

Joh. 14. 16. Let that reviving Comforter
Eph. 1. 13. Seal to us pardning Grace ;
I∫a. 59. 2. Nor let the Sins we loath, eclipse
The Lu∫tre of thy Face.

1 John 2. 1. Behold our Glorious Advocate
At thy right Hand inthron'd,
Heb. 9. 26. Who by the Offering of his Blood
Has for them all aton'd.

He for our great and numerous Sins
Once numerous Torments bore ;
I∫a 53. 3, 4. For them the Scourges, Thorns, and Nails,
His Fle∫h so rudely tore.

Rivers

Rivers of Blood ran from his Wounds,   *Pf.* 22. 14.
   His Eyes wept briny Show'rs;   *Heb.* 5. 7.
And all this Pain and Grief he felt
   For Crimes intirely ours.   *Ifa.*53.5,6.

LORD, fince our Pardon coft fo dear,   1 *Pet.* 1.
   Yet comes to us fo free,   18, 19.
Whence is it that our narrow Souls
   Shew no more Love to Thee?

May this Endearing Love of thine,   *Luke* 7. 47.
   By thoufand Torments prov'd,
Increafe our Love and Zeal to Thee,   1*Cor.*6.20.
   Who us fo much haft lov'd.

H Y M N XXIX.

[*As the* 100 *Pfalm.*]
ETernal Father, how Divine,
   How Noble is this Gift of thine!
That thou fhouldft fend thy only Son,   *Rom.*3.22.
That Holy, Lov'd, and Lovely One;   *Mat.* 3 17.

The nobleft Object of thy Love,   *Prov* 8.31.
To leave his Throne and Crown above,   *Phil.* 2. 6,
To dwell with Mortals here below,   7, 8.
And Death for them to undergo!

And Thou, bleft Saviour, who didft come   *Prov* 8 31.
So freely from thy Heav'nly Home,   *Pfal* 46.
To make thy Self a Sacrifice   6, 7, 8.
For Criminals and Enemies:
      D 3   How

How full of Wonder is that Love
Joh. 17.5. That could determine thee to move
From thy Illustrious Palace, where
The Heav'nly Host did Thee revere !

*Isa.*6.com- Where Flaming *Seraphs* bow'd before
par'd with Thy awful Scepter, to adore
John 12. Thy *Holy Holy, Holy* Name,
37—42. And thy Perfections to proclaim !

Love made thee all this Glory leave,
*Heb.*10.20 A Veil of Human Flesh receive,
Isa. 53. To live in Grief and Misery,
And after all to bleed and die !

Gal 3. 13. To die a Death the most accurst,
Phil. 2.8. And of all Deaths the very worst ;
Mat. 27. To be with lingring Torments slain,
28——31 Abus'd with Scoffs and vile Disdain !

All this Thou hast endur'd, that we
1 *Cor.* 1. Holy and Happy too might be,
30. And with Thee in thy Kingdom reign,
Rev. 20.6. When Thou, dear LORD, shalt come again.

HYMN

H Y M N XXX.

YOU that the Holy JESUS love,   *Cant.* 1. 4]
  Give Honour to his Name;
The great Atchievements of his Grace
  In thankful Verse proclaim.

Tho what your highest Thoughts surmounts
  Can never be exprest;   *Eph.* 3. 18,
Yet something of it you may tell,   19.
  And wonder out the rest.

Remember all his mighty Deeds,
  His Sorrows all review;   *Phil.* 2. 6,
How he abas'd his Glorious Self,   7, 8.
  To bleed and die for you.

Remember all the Shame and Scorn,
  The Vinegar and Gall,   *Pf.* 69. 21.
The gaping Wounds thro which he pour'd *Mat.* 27.
  His Vital Juices all.

His Sorrows, as his Vertues, were   *Cant.* 5.
  Innumerable found;   9, &c.
Troubles from Earth, from Heaven and Hell, *Ifa.* 53. 3.
  His spotless Soul surround.

Crucify'd by the worst of Men,   *Acts* 3 13,
  Forsaken by the best,   14, 15.
With th' endless Number of our Sins,   *Mat.* 26.
  Sin's mighty Weight oppress'd.   56.
          Pf. 40. 12.

            D 4   He

Gal. 3. 13. He felt the Curfes of the Law,
Mat. 27. His Father's Wrath fuftain'd;
46.   Endur'd the cruel fhock of all
Luke 22 The Powers of Hell unchain'd.
53
Acts 1. 9, But after all victorious prov'd,
20,   In Triumph did afcend,
2*Tim.*4. 8 And now prepares us Crowns and Thrones,
Rev. 3.21. And Joys that ne'er fhall end.

H Y M N XXXI.

[*As the* 25 *Pfalm.*]

LORD, Thou haft treated us
   With true and living Bread;
John 6.32,
33, 34. Thy Body, as upon the Crofs,
   The painful Crofs, it bled.

Mat 26. Thy Blood's a precious Wine,
27, 28. The Heart of God it chears;
*Judg.*9.13. With Heav'nly Sweets, and Joys Divine,
Rom. 8. It calms our guilty Fears.
33, 34.

   A Living Spring thy Side,
*Joh.*19.34. Thy pierc'd Side did impart,
Pf. 22. 14. Thro which a vital Juice did glide
   Down from thy melting Heart.

*Pf.*22 16. This Crimfon Stream, with thofe
   Thy Hands and Feet did yield,
*Zech.*13.1. A Bath for Sinners does compofe,
   In which they're cleans'd and heal'd.

          Such

Such Bleſſings, LORD, in Thee,
  If at thy Croſs we meet,   *Mat.* 26.
What Joys will in thy Kingdom be,   29.
  Joys how Divinely Sweet!

When thou with Glory crown'd,   *Rev.* 3.21.
  Thy Saints on Thrones wilt place,
And ſatiate all thy Gueſts around
  With th'Viſion of thy Face.   1 *Joh.*3.2.

From that bleſt Paradiſe   *Rev.*22 3.
  None e'er ſhall be exil'd;   & 20. 10,
None by a Serpent's tempting Voice, 14.
  Of Joy and Life beguil'd.

The Tree of Life ſhall chaſe   *Rev.* 22 2.
  Death thence, and all its Fears; & 22. 1.
Rivers of Pleaſure there have place,
  And there are none of Tears.   & 21. 4.

H Y M N XXXII.

[*As the* 100 *Pſalm.*]
LET all who love our Saviour's Name, *Cant.* 1.
  That Name ſo full of Heav'nly Grace, 3, 4.
In Songs of Triumph ſpread his Fame
Thro every Age, and every Place.

He kindly laid aſide his Crown,   *Phil.* 2. 6,
And Robes of awful Majeſty ;   7, 8.
And in a Servant's Form came down
To bear a Croſs, and on it die.

                      With

Heb. 5.7.
Luk. 22.44 With Tears, and Sweat, and Blood imbru'd,
Isa. 53. 7. This Holy Lamb was sacrific'd;
Mat. 27. Jeer'd by the barbarous Multitude,
40—44   And by profaner Priests despis'd.

1 *Cor.* 15. But dying thus, he pluck'd the Sting
54—57.   From Death; and rising from the Grave,
Job 18.14. He triumph'd o'er the mighty *King*
Heb. 2. 14. *Of Terrors,* as a Captive Slave.

Acts 1. 9, Then to his Heav'nly Throne was rais'd,
10.   Whence he'll descend again, to be
Phil. 2. 9, Thro the whole World ador'd and prais'd
10, 11.   By every Tongue, and every Knee.

Tho Tears, and Blood, and Spittle here
Clouded, profan'd, and marr'd his Face,
Rev. 1.16. The Mid-day Sun is not so clear,
Now 'tis adorn'd with Heavenly Grace.

Rev. 5.   Angelick Songs his Beauties praise,
9, &c.   While, clad in glorious Robes of Light,
Mat. 17.2. He darts innumerable Rays
1 *Tim.* 6. Around, for mortal Eyes too bright.
   16.
Ezek. 16. This Glory *Adam's* Sons partake,
5——15. Who once deform'd and odious were;
1 *Joh.*1.7. For that pure Blood he shed, can make
A Leprous Sinner clean and fair.

2 *Cor.* 5. 4. Our Bodies too he will refine;
Phil. 3.21. Vile Bodies, under which we groan,
Shall with Immortal Beauty shine,
Render'd all lovely like his Own.

HYMN

H Y M N XXXIII.

WHat wondrous things we now behold 1 *Tim.* 3.
    At this Mysterious Board ! 16.
What copious Matter for a Song *Gal.* 3. 1.
    Of Praises they afford ! *Mat.* 26.
                             30.

Extended on a Cross we see
    The Lord whom we adore,
Both giving and receiving Wounds, *Col.* 2. 15.
    Bath'd in triumphant Gore.

No Victor's Robe so rich a Dye *Isa.* 63. 1.
    Before did ever stain,
No Champion such a Victory *Heb.* 2. 14,
    Before did ever gain. 15.

Glory and Strength his Torments add
    To all his mighty Deeds ; *Heb.* 2. 10.
His Enemies fly, and fall the more,
    The more he groans and bleeds.

Tho the Law's Curse lights on his Head, *Gal.* 3. 13.
    While Satan wounds his Heel, *Gen.* 3. 15.
His Body's bruis'd by Men, his Heart 1 *Cor.* 15,
    Death's cruel Sting does feel ; 56.

Yet with firm Courage he o'er all
    Bears up his Conquering Head,
Till on their Captive Necks his Feet *Col.* 2. 14,
    In solemn Triumph tread. 15.

This

Isa. 63. 3.
Heb. 10.   This Shock our Lord suftain'd Alone,
12,13, 14.   But makes us fhare the Spoils ;
Mat. 27.   He felt his Father's dreadful Frowns,
45   That we might have his Smiles.

Rom. 8 15.
Ift. 1. 6.   To cure our Wounds and putrid Sores,
& 53. 5.   Was pierc'd in every Limb ;
Gal. 3 13   His Crofs, our Tree of Life, became
& 4. 4, 5.   A Tree of Death to him.

Rev. 1. 18. But tho once Dead, He's now Alive,
                 And lives for evermore :
2 *Tim.* 3.   Then let his Saints, whofe Life is hid
12.   In Chrift, his Name adore.

H Y M N XXXIV.

[*As the* 100 *Pfalm.*]

1 *Pet.* 2. 3.   COME let us all, who here have feen,
                 And tafted of our Saviour's Grace,
                 From his bleft Table to his Crofs,
                 In Thought, his weary Footfteps trace.

Luk. 23. 33 Let's trace Him up to *Calvary*,
                 Not leave him as his Followers did,
Mat. 26.   Who having at his Table fup'd,
56.   Forfook their fuffering Lord, and fled.

John 18 1. Into the Garden firft he goes,
Mat 26.   Where Mortal Fears befet him round ;
38   Sin's prefling Weight o'erwhelms his Soul,
Mark 14   And finks his Body to the Ground.
5.   Here

Here, proftrate as he lies, he groans,
Pouring out Pray'rs with fervent Cries,
Till he fweats Diops of Blood, to mix   *Luk.*22.44
With Floods that iffue from his Eyes.   *Heb.* 5. 7.

Yet are his Sorrows but begun,   *Mat.* 26.
By one Difciple he's betray'd,   48.
Another Him with Oaths denies,   *Ver.*69,&c
The reft all run like Sheep afraid.   *Ver.*31,56.

Falfly accus'd, he's doom'd to die ;   *Ver.*59,60.
Loaded with·Blafphemy and Scorn,   *Ver.* 66,
He's rudely buffeted and bound,   67, 68.
His Sacred Flefh with Scourges torn.   *Mat.* 27.2.
    Ver. 26.

His Temples wear a Wreath of Thorns,
Spittle his reverend Face profanes ;   *Ver.* 29.
His weary Shoulders bear a Crofs,   *John* 19.
On which he fuffers Mortal Pains.   17, 18.

Between two Thieves he lingring dies,   *Mat.* 27.
While thoufand Tortures on him meet ;   38.
His Heart's diffolv'd within, his Blood   *Pfal.* 22.
Flows out in Streams from Hands and Feet. 14,15, 16.

Thefe Streams, join'd with that other Flood *John* 19.
That gufh'd out from his wounded Side,   34.
Compofe a Sovereign Bath, wherein   *Zech.*13.1.
The Leprous Soul is purify'd.

HYMN

Hymn XXXV.

Pſal. 65.4. **H**Appy are they our LORD has choſe
        In his bleſt Courts to dwell,
      His Praiſes ſtill their Thoughts employ,
Pſal. 29.9.   Their Tongues his Glory tell.

Pſal. 27. 4. There He his Lovelineſs makes known
        To all who love his Name;
Iſa. 28. 5. To them He is a glorious Crown,
       And beauteous Diadem.

Pſal. 23.5. With a Celeſtial Banquet there
       His Table's richly ſpread;
Luke 22.   The Wine's the Tincture of his Veins,
19, 20.   His Body is the Bread.

Cant. 5. 1. To entertain his happy Friends,
Pſal. 23.5. He oft repeats his Call;
Mat. 22. Pours fragrant Oil upon their Heads,
11, 12.   Gives Robes to clothe 'em all.

Iſa. 57.15. Nay, every contrite Mind to him
Pſ. 51. 17. A Holy Temple proves:
      For humble Souls are his Delight,
       And He *dwells* where he *loves.*

      He at the Door of every Heart
Rev. 3.20. Does friendly Calls renew;
      " Open to Me, and you ſhall ſup
       " With Me, and I with you.

Ant

And will the High and Lofty One   *Iſa.* 57. 15.
   Vouchſafe to dwell with Men?
Open Eternal Doors, and let   *Pſal.* 24.
   The King of Glory in.   7, &c.

This Entertainment, LORD, of Thine,   1 *Pet.* 1.
   So gen'rous and ſo free,   18, 19.
Coſt many a Pang, and many a Groan,
   And many a Wound to Thee.

Eternal Praiſe to thy Great Name,   *Revel.* 5.
   By all the Hoſt of Heaven,   9, &c.
By every Nation, every Tongue,
   And every Heart be given.

H Y M N XXXVI.

[*As the* 100 *Pſalm.*]

WHAT mighty Conqueror do we ſee,
   Whoſe Garments are diſtain'd *Iſa.* 63.
                 (with Blood,
Whoſe rich Apparel ſeems to be
All tinctur'd in a Crimſon Flood?

Like one who has the Winepreſs trod,   *Ver.* 2.
Whoſe Clothes the Grape has purpl'd o'er?
'Tis the *Eternal* Son of God,   *Iſa.* 53. 5.
All full of Wounds, all ſtain'd with Gore.

A *Mighty Conqueror* indeed,
Who conquers by receiving Blows;
To give Wounds, is content to bleed;   *Heb.* 2. 14,
And by his Death ſubdues his Foes.   15.

                         He

He treads 'em down, tho all Alone,
Iſa. 63. 3.   And with their Blood his Veſture's ſtain'd,
But firſt is all bath'd in his own,
His own by many a Wound is drain'd.

Col. 2. 15.   His Blood Hell's ſubtile Powers confounds,
To them a Mortal Liquor proves;
Luke 10.   But is a Balm to heal our Wounds,
34.   A Wine to chear the Souls he loves.

Joh. 19. 34.   The Veſſels that contain'd this Juice,
& 20. 25.   A Spear and ruder Nails did broach;
And while his Fleſh they pierce and bruiſe,
Pſ. 69. 20.   His Heart is broken with Reproach.

Iſa. 53. 5.   But bruis'd, and broke, and mangled thus,
This Sacrifice our Pardon gain'd;
Mat. 26.   And thus prepar'd, is Food to us,
26, 27.   By which we live, and are ſuſtain'd.

Pſ. 78. 24.   Thrice happy they, whoſe Tents around
Pſ. 116. 13.   Such Heavenly Bleſſings ſtill are ſpread'
John 6.   Whoſe Cup is with Salvation crown'd,
31, 32, 33.   Their Board with True and Living Bread'

Rom. 5. 20.   Praiſe Him whoſe Mercies know no end,
2 Chron.   But to a vaſter Sum ariſe
28. 9.   Than Sins themſelves; for *theſe* extend
Pſ. 108. 4.   To Heaven, but *thoſe* above the Skies.

HYMN

H Y M N XXXVII.

[*As the* 100 *Pfalm.*]

OThers may tell of famous things
Done by their Heroes and their Kings;
The LORD we ferve, them all exceeds   *Rom.* 5.
For mighty Sufferings, mighty Deeds.   7, 8.

The Torments he has undergone,   *1 Pet.* 1.
The glorious Trophies he has won,   12.
Armies of wondring Angels caufe   *Rev.* 5.
To fill the Heavens with loud Applaufe.   11, 12.

Deep in our Breafts let us record   *1 Cor.* 11.
The Story of our Dying LORD :   24,25, 26.
As we his kind Memorials view,   *Mat.* 26.
Our Wonder, and our Songs renew.   30

From Heaven the *Lord of Glory* came,   *Jam* 2. 1.
On Earth to bear Reproach and Shame ;   *Ifa.* 50 6.
The Son of God his Face to veil;   *John* 1.14.
Affumes a Body weak and frail.

  Rev. 19.16
The *King of Kings* a Crown adorns,   *Ifa.* 6 3.
Inftead of Gems, all fet with Thorns :   compar'd
He whom the Angels prais'd and bleft,   with *John*
Is made the Rabble's Scorn and Jeft.   12.41.

The *Meek*, the *Juft*, the *Holy One*   *Mat.* 21.5;
Under the Weight of Sin does groan.   *Aĉts* 3 14,
The Prince of Life would learn to die,   15.
And be as Low as he was High.   *Phil.* 2. 6,
  7, 8.

E   H.

1 *Tim.* 4.8. He that diftributes Crowns and Thrones,
*Rev.*3. 21. Hangs on a Tree, and bleeds, and groans:
*Act.*10.39. He on a Crofs refigns his Breath,
*Rev.*1. 18. Who keeps the Keys of Hell and Death.

   'Twas thus, becaufe he'd have it fo,
Joh. 10 11 That we his Wondrous Love might know:
Mat. 26. To refcue us, he was betray'd ;
48,49,50. To make us free, a Pris'ner made ;

Pf. 22.15. To raife us, in the Duft did roll ,
*Ifa.*53.4,5. Bore many Wounds, to make us whole:
   To give us Pleafure, felt our Pain ;
Rom 6.23. And dy'd, that we might Life obtain.

1 *Cor.* 15. Thus Sin, Death, and the Powers of Hell,
54—57. Conquer'd, difarm'd, and wounded fell.
Col. 2. 15. He mounted then his Throne above,
Eph. 4. 8. And conquers Sinners by his Love.
2*Cor* 5.20.
   LORD, fince our Pardon, and our Blifs,
1*Cor.*6.20. Were bought at fuch a Price as this ;
1 *Cor.* 7. As Thou art ours, we're Thine alone ;
22, 23. Thine will we be, and not our own

           HYMN

H Y M N XXXVIII.

WHen Chriſt, at *Simon's* Table plac'd, *Luke* 7.
   His ſacred Doctrine taught ;   36, 37, 38.
A Penitent behind him ſtood,
   Whom Love had thither brought.

She with Devotion kiſs'd his Feet,
   Bath'd 'em with flowing Eyes,
Then drys 'em with her ſpreading Locks,
   And fragrant Oil applies.

'Twas Love theſe Funeral Tears prepar'd   *Ver.* 47.
   Before her LORD was dead ;   *Mat.* 26.
Officious Love ſupply'd the Balm   12.
   Before his Wounds had bled.

Her Faith the Virtue of his Blood
   Apply'd, before 'twas ſpilt ;
To waſh her Soul from every Stain,   *1 John* 1. 7.
   And expiate her Guilt.

The Saviour's ſympathizing Heart
   Her pious Sorrow feels,
Commends her Faith, her Love applauds, *Ver.* 47, 50.
   His pard'ning Grace reveals.

Thus every Soul ſucceeds, that bows
   At the Redeemer's Feet,
Thoſe who repent, believe and love,
   Chriſt at his Table meet.

E 2   The

Rom. 5. 20, The Motions of thy Sovereign Grace,
    25.   LORD, let no Sin controul ;
          Forgiving Glances from thy Eyes
          Will ravish every Soul.

          These Faithful Pledges of thy Love
          Declare Thee still the same :
Luk. 22. 19 For these Memorials of thy Cross
          We praise thy Sacred Name.

H Y M N XXXIX.

[*As the* 100 *Psalm.*]

Gal. 2. 20. COME let us go and die with Him,
          Who was content to die for us ;
Isa. 53. 5, 6. Let's wound and crucify those Sins
          That nail'd our Saviour to his Cross

2 Co. 7. 11. May Holy Indignation raise
          A Just Revenge in every Breast !
Pl. 97. 10. May every Soul, that JESUS loves,
          The very Thoughts of Sin detest !

Rom. 2. 8, 9. Hence all ye viprous Brood of Vice,
          That bring a Train of endless Woes ,
          O how I loath and hate you now,
          As mine and as my Saviour's Foes !

    2. 23. Yours are the bloody Hands that seiz'd,
          That bound, that buffeted, that slew
       14, The *Lord of Life*, and on the Cross
    15.   Your poison'd Arrows at him threw.

                           You

You are the barbarous Enemies,   *Luk.*19 14.
Who ſtill refuſe that Chriſt ſhould reign;   *Ver* 27.
Juſtice demands you ſhould be drag'd   *Numb.* 15.
Without the Camp, and there be ſlain.   35.
                                     Heb. 13.

Hence all your vain deluding Arts,   11,12, 13.
Which the unwary Soul beguile;   *Heb.* 3. 13.
Theſe have no charms for one that ſees *Gal.* 6. 4.
Redeeming Mercy on him ſmile.

My Robes, when waſh'd in ſacred Blood, *Rev.*7. 13,
Shall I again with Blots deface?   14.
My Soul, by Grace advanc'd to Heav'n, *Ch.* 3 4.
Shall I again to Hell debaſe?   *Luke* 10.
                                     15.

Prevent me, O Almighty Grace!
Nor let me e'er ſo treacherous prove,
To crucify my LORD afreſh,   *Heb.* 6. 6.
And render Hate for all his Love!   *Pſ.* 109. 4,
                                     5.

His Life the Model be of mine;   1 *Pet.* 2.
His Word the Rule to guide my Ways; 21, 22.
His Croſs the Death of all my Crimes; *Col.* 3. 16.
His Love the Subject of my Praiſe.   *Rom* 6. 6,
                                    *Rev.*5.8.---

HYMN XL.

*Heb.*12.22. LET all, who enter *Sion's* Gate,
*Pf.*100. 4. And in God's sacred Courts attend,
Heb. 4. 16 Praise him before his Holy Seat,
Eph. 3. 18, Whose Mercy knows no Bounds or End.
19.
Pf. 103.1. To the Soul's inward Harmony
Pf. 100. 1. Join the sweet Musick of the Tongue ;
1 *Cor.* 14. No jarring Thought admitted be,
15.   No Mind untun'd, no Heart unstrung.
Col. 3. 16.

*Rom.*8.32. Praise Him, who did not spare to send
     From Heaven his own Eternal Son,
*Heb.*10.20 To veil himself in Flesh, and end
*Ifa.*53.2,3. That Life in Blood which Tears begun.

John 1.18. Praise that Redeemer, who forsook
Phil. 2.6, The Bosom of his Father's Love ,
7, 8.   The Guilt of Sinners on him took,
2*Cor.*5.21. The Pain without the Crime to prove.
*Ifa.*53.5,6,
Mat 3 16. And praise that bright Immortal Dove,
Pf. 14. 3. Who contrite Hearts with Joy inspires,
Rom. 5. 5. And sheds abroad Redeeming Love,
     To warm our Breasts with holy Fires.

1 *Joh* 5.7. O praise the Sacred *Three* in *One,*
     To whose Love, Wisdom, Pow'r, we owe
2*Tim.*1.10 That Bliss which is in Time begun,
     But shall with Time no period know.

HYMN

H Y M N XLI.

THE Sun of Righteoufnefs has fhin'd, *Mal.* 4. 2.
And God's new Cov'nant has reveal'd , *Luke* 1.78.
Chrift's Hand the facred Bond has fign'd, *Heb.* 8. 6.
His Blood the facred Bond has feal'd.   *Pf.*40.6,7.
                                                                          *Luk.*22.20

His numerous Promifes affure
Salvation on his Father's part :   *2Cor.*1.20.
Salvation can't but be fecure,   *Heb.*9. 13,
When purchas'd with his bleeding Heart. 14, 15.

The kind Teftator freely dies,   *Ver.*16,17.
To ratify this Teftament :
The Sacred Dove from Glory flies,   *Mat.*3.16.
To gain the Sinner's free Confent.   *John* 16.
                                                                          7 — 16.

The Table of the LORD difplays
The Dear Memorials of his Love ;   *Luk* 22.19
The Church below applauds his Grace,   *Rev.* 7.
In Confort with the Church above.   9 — 15.

LORD, when we gave our felves to Thee, 2 *Cor.*8. 5.
Drawn by the charming Bands of Love,   *Hof.* 11.4.
We vow'd for ever Thine to be,   1*Pet* 3.21.
And by thy Grace will Conftant prove.

Thee we have always Gracious found,   *Pfal.* 36.
Thy Promifes are firm and true :   5 — 8.
The Tyes wherewith our Souls are bound, *Pfal.* 119.
We now moft folemnly renew.   106.

E 4   Command,

Acts 9. 6.　Command, and we'll obey thy Call,
Mark 8.　　We'll take our Cross, and follow Thee
34, 35　　To Prison, to the Judgment Hall,
Joh 18. 15.　Without the Gate to *Calvary*.
Ch. 19. 26,

27.　　　Since Thou art ours, may we retain
Cant. 2 16.　Thy Sacred Image which we bear:
Col. 3 19　Since we are thine, may we remain
Pf. 119. 38　Ever devoted to thy Fear

1 Chron. 29　Our selves to Thee, LORD, we resign,
10 — 18.　All we possess to Thee belongs,
Pf. 56 12.　Thou hast our Vows, our Hearts are thine,
　　　　And Thou shalt ever have our Songs.

H Y M N XLII.

[*As the* 100 *Pfalm.*]

COME let us bless the Glorious Name
Mat. 1 22,　　Of our Great Prince *Immanuel*,
23.　　Who from Heaven's highest Regions came,
Pf 86. 13.　To save us from the lowest Hell.

Acts 3. 15　Nor did this *Prince of Life* disdain
1 Tim 3 16　A mortal Body to assume,
Ifa. 53. 3, 4　To live in sorrow, die in pain,
Mat. 27.　And he inter'd within a Tomb.
60

Rom 5. 21.　That Men, by Guilt of Life bereav'd,
　　　　Might have their num'rous Crimes forgiven;
Rom. 5 10.　Rebels might be to Grace receiv'd,
Feb. 12　T' inlarge the Family of Heaven.
3 , 23.　　　　　　　　　　　　Th'An-

Th'Angelick Hoſt this Grace admire,   *1 Pet.*1 12.
Which reconciles Apoſtate Man ;
To ſound that Myſtick Deep deſire,   *Heb.* 9. 5.
Contriv'd before the World began.   *Eph.*1 4,5.

They with ſoft Muſick fill'd the Air,   *Luk.*2. 13,
When firſt our Saviour drew his Breath :   14.
They chear'd his mind oppreſt with Care, *Mat* 4. 11.
When *tempted*, and approaching Death. *Luk.*22.43

They now around his Throne above   *Rev.* 5.11,
To Heav'nly Ayres their Voices raiſe ;   12.
With humble Joy that Grace approve   *Rev.* 7.11,
Which yields 'em endleſs Songs of Praiſe. 12.

While they loud *Hallelujah*'s ſing   *Rev.* 19 1.
Above our Notes, our Thoughts above ;
In glad *Hoſanna*'s to our King   *Mat* 21. 9.
We'll ſing of Reconciling Love.

HYMN XLIII.

BEhold the Saviour of the World
  Embru'd with *Sweat* and *Gore*,   *Mat.* 27.
Expiring on that ſhameful Croſs,
  Where he our Sorrows bore !

Compaſſion for loſt Human Race   *Heb.* 2. 14,
  Brought down Heav'n's only Son,   15,16,&c.
To veil in fleſh his radiant Face,   *Heb.* 1, 3.
  And for their Sins atone.

Who

Who can to love his Name forbear,
1 *Pet.* 1.   That of his Sufferings hears,
18, 19.   And finds the Ransom of his Soul
Was Blood as well as Tears?

*Act.*20.28. Thy Sacred Blood, O Son of God!
Which ran from many a Wound;
*Pf.*22.12, When Earth's and Hell's malicious Pow'r,
13.   All compafs'd thee around:

Till Death's pale Enfigns o'er thy Cheeks
*Joh.*19.30. And trembling Lips were fpread;
Till Light forfook thy dying Eyes,
And Life thy drooping Head.

Ifa. 53.4, Joy for thy Torments we receive,
5.   Life in thy Death have found;
*Rev.*7.14, For the Reproaches of thy Crofs
15, &c.   Shall be with Glory crown'd.

1 *Joh.*4 19 May we a grateful Senfe retain
Of thy Redeeming Love!
1 *John* 3.3. And live *below* like thofe that hope
To live with Thee *above!*

HYMN

HYMN XLIV.

WHile thy Love's Pledges we receive *1 Cor. 11.*
   In this blest Supper, LORD, we see 26.
What grateful Tribute, what Returns *Pfal.* 116.
Of Love and Praise we owe to Thee. 12.

O may thy Altar's holy Fire *Ifa. 6. 5,*
Inflame our Hearts, refine our Tongues! 6, 7.
May Love Divine our Breasts infpire *Cant.* 1. 3,
With Heav'nly Thoughts, and Heav'nly 4.
                    (Songs !

Tho to extol thy Wondrous Grace *Eph.* 3. 18,
OurThoughts andWords too low will prove, 19.
Thou, LORD, wilt ne'er refufe a Song *Job* 37.
From any Heart that's tun'd with Love. 19, 20.

While to thy Crofs we turn our Eyes,
And there thy Agonies review ; *Ifa.* 53. 4,
What we deferv'd, but Thou haft born, 5, 6.
Thy Wounds, thy Groans, thy Torments
                    (fhew.

While Terror o'er thy Soul was fpread,
Thy cruel Foes reviling ftood ; - *Mat.* 27.
While Clouds of Wrath burft on thyHead, 39.
They bath'd their Hands in Sacred Blood. *Ifa.* 53. 10.

The Sun aftonifh'd hid his Face, *Mat.* 27.
The Heavens a fable Garment wore ; 45.
The frighted Earth's Foundations fhook, *Ver.* 51,
And folid Rocks afunder tore :
               The

The Temple's Veil was rent, to shew
  Heav'ns Throne unveil'd to our High
                    (Priest,
Disclosing Graves, and rising Saints,
  The Virtue of his Death contest.

Thou, LORD of Life, didst soon revive;
  Nor could thy Tomb Thee long retain,
Who to lay down thy Life hadst pow'r,
  And pow'r to take it up again.

Thy Body, once with Wounds deform'd,
  Does now with Heav'nly Glory shine,
Adorn'd, and made a Temple fit
  For such a beauteous Soul as thine.

As once upon the cursed Tree
  Our Sins, with Thee our Saviour, dy'd:
So, LORD, we hope to rise like Thee,
  And sing thy Triumphs at thy Side.

H Y M M   XLV.

HOW glorious is this Holy Place,
  Where Bread of Life is giv'n!
This surely is the House of God!
  This is the Gate of Heav'n!

JESUS, the Master of the Feast,
  Vouchsafes his Presence here;
The *Cup of Blessing* passes round,
  The pious Guests to chear.

                              Dainties

Dainties that Royal Tables bear,   *Cant.* 1
    And Bowls of ruddy Wine,   *Pſ.* 5. 5.
Can't with this Nobler Board compare,
    Crown'd with a Feaſt Divine.

Hence faithleſs Doubts, deſponding Fears *Mat* 3 2.
    No more our Joys moleſt :   *Luke* 7 17.
Hence all vain Thoughts, and vile Deſires &c.
    No more our Souls infeſt.   *Rom.* 5 2.

Can Sinners doubt their Pardon, when
    Their Judg upon 'em ſmiles ?   *Eph.* 5. 2.
Can they ungratefully rebel
    Whom JESUS reconciles ?   *Rom* 2

The Merit of his Blood can calm   *Heb* 9 2
    The Soul with Guilt oppreſt,
The Torments of his Croſs can make   *Ch* 5 14.
    The Soul all Sin deteſt.

JESUS, we lift our Hearts to Thee,   *John* 2
    To Thee our longing Eyes,   14, 15
To Thee our ſolemn Vows addreſs,   *Zech.* 12
    To Thee our ardent Cries.   10.

O may our Sins, that made Thee bleed,   *Gal.* 2.
    All on thy Croſs expire !
O may the Joys, thy Banquet gives,   *Pſ.* 36. 2
    Equal our warm Deſire !   *Can.* 2
                  4

So ſhall we mount upon the Wings
    Of chearful Hope and Love,
And here begin the Songs that we   *Rev* 7.
    Shall better ſing above.

HYMN

H Y M N XLVI.

ʃ

Y̌E happy Guests, who meet around
    This Table, your Oblations bring;
Pf. 50.23. Here every one's a Prieft, who has
1 *Pet.* 2.5. A Heart to love, and Tongue to fing.

Eph. 5. 2. Our Saviour's bleeding Sacrifice
Heb. 13. His boundlefs Love and Grace difplays,
15,16.   As a juft Homage, he demands
           Our Sacrifice of Love and Praife.

Rev. 1. 5. 'Twas Love expos'd him to Reproach,
              To unexampled Grief and Pain :
1 *Joh.* 3 16 Lefs Power than that of Love Divine,
*Joh.*15.13. Nor *would* nor *could* his Crofs fuftain.

Mat. 26. See him abandon'd by his Friends;
56.   By a perfidious Kifs betray'd ,
V. 48, 49 Sold as a defpicable Slave;
Luke 22. With Swords and Staves a Pris'ner made.
4, 5, 47.
V. 57.   See him to the Tribunal led,
V. 59,60. There charg'd with Crimes by Men fub-
Luke 23.   (orn'd,
Mat. 14. By Princes and by Priefts condemn'd,
65.   And by the vileft Wretches fcorn'd.
Heb. 1. 6.

           That Awful Face, which low Refpect
           From proftrate Angels did command,
Mat. 27. Spat on by Men of fervile ftate,
27——30.   And ftruck by each rude Soldier's hand.

                                          Bearing

Bearing his Cross to *Golgotha,*	*John* 19.
With labouring steps behold him go;	16, 17.
And from his Wounds, when open'd there,	*Pf.* 22. 16.
O fee what crimfon Rivers flow !	*Joh.* 19. 34.

Plung'd in thefe Streams, our guilty Souls	1 *Joh.* 1. 7.
Purg'd from their numerous Sins fhall be :	
Juftice and Mercy, tho provok'd	*Rom.* 3. 26.
By us, O LORD, are pleas'd with Thee.	*Mat.* 3. 17.

O Lamb of God ! who bor'ft our Guilt,	*Joh.* 1. 29.
To thee immortal Praife belongs :	*Rev.* 7. 11,
While we thy Love and Sufferings fing,	12.
Angels fhall hear, and join their Songs.	*Luke* 2.
	13, 14.

HYMN

H Y M N XLVII.

*Mat.*1.21. JESUS ! O Word Divinely fweet !
Ifa. 52. 7, How charming is the Sound !
8, 9.   What joyful News ! what Heavenly Senfe
        In that dear Name is found !

*Rom.*3.23. Our Souls were guilty, and condemn'd
Eph. 2.12.   In hopelefs Fetters lay ;
Rom. 3.   Our Souls with numerous Sins deprav'd,
10—19.   To Death and Hell a Prey.

Col. 1. 14. Jefus, to purge away this Guilt,
        A willing Victim fell ;
Col. 2. 14, And on his Crofs Triumphant broke
15.   The Bands of Death and Hell.

Heb. 2.14, Our Foes were mighty to deftroy,
15.   He mightier was to fave :
Acts 2.   He dy'd, but could not long be held
24—28.   A Pris'ner in the Grave.

Heb. 7. 25. JESUS ! who mighty art to fave,
    · Still pufh thy Conquefts on ;
    Extend the Triumphs of thy Crofs
Mal 1.11. Where'er the Sun has fhone.

Heb. 2.10. O Captain of Salvation ! make
        Thy Power and Mercy known :
Pfal. 110. That Crouds of willing Converts may
1, 2, 3.   Worfhip before thy Throne.

Hymn XLVIII.

[_As the 100 Psalm._]

(prove

THOU haft o'ercome: LORD, who can   2 _Cor._ 5.
  Invincible to Heav'nly Love?   14, 15.
My conquer'd Soul I muft refign   _Pf._ 45. 2.
To that victorious Arm of Thine.   3, 4, 5.

Thy Grace, whofe wondrous Pow'r imparts
The tend'reft Senfe to flinty Hearts,   _Acts_ 2. 37.
My inmoft Soul with Love infpires,   1 _John_ 4.
And mixes Joy with pure Defires.   9, 10.

For who, my LORD, can love like Thee? _Eph._ 3. 18.
Whofe Love was e'er fo Great, fo Free? 19.
Angels may well admire the Flame,   1 _Pet._ 2. 3.
But they have never felt the fame.

Nor Men whom Nature has ally'd,   _Rom._ 5, 6.
Or, ftricteft Bonds of Friendfhip ty'd;   7, 8.
Who ever did his Life expofe,
To ranfom his ungrateful Foes?   _Ver._ 10.

But Thou, O Son of God, didft take
Frail human Nature for our fake;   _Phil._ 2. 7.
The Griefs of human Life didft try,   _Ifa._ 53. 4.
And on a Crofs for Rebels die.

This Offering well deferves that We   _Rom._ 12. 1.
Should facrifice our Selves to Thee;
And where we owe fo vaft a Debt,   _Ch._ 14. 7.
To pay our Homage ne'er forget.   8, 9.

F   To

*Act.*17.28. To Thee, in whom we live and move,
*Gal.*2. 20. We give our Praife, we give our Love ;
Ifa. 53. 6. To Thee, on whom our Sins were laid,
Eph. 1. 7. Whofe Blood was for our Pardon paid.

Rev 1. 6. To Thee, who mak'ft us Priefts and Kings;
  Priefts to attend on Holy Things,
*1 Pet.*2 5. And Kings to reign with Thee above,
& *ver.* 9. In Realms of Blifs and endlefs Love.

HYMN XLIX.

[*As the* 100 *Pfalm.*]
*Joh.*19.30 'TIS *finifh'd,* the Redeemer crys,
  Then lowly bows his fainting Head,
And foon th' expiring Sacrifice
Sinks to the Regions of the Dead.

'Tis done—The mighty Work is done !
Heb. 1. For Men or Angels much too Great,
Which None, but GOD's Eternal Son,
Or would attempt, or could compleat.
  (Wounds,
'Tis done,—His Tears, his Groans, and
His Sweat and Blood, his Pains and Toils,
Heb. 2. 9. Vict'ry with Deathlefs Glory crowns,
Col. 2.14, With Trophys, and Triumphant Spoils.
15.
Heb. 2 14, Hell's broken Troops find no Defence,
15. Sin dies, and Death it felf is flain :
*1Cor.*15.54 Hope, Peace, Love, Joy and Innocence
55,56,57. Return to dwell on Earth again.
Gal. 5.22.   The

The Conqueror falls a Sacrifice,   *Pf.*40.6,7.
Heav'n's juft Refentments to appeafe:
Juftice with Mercy now complys,   *Pf.* 85.10.
Both with the Sinner's Pardon pleas'd.   *Rom* 3.26.

'Iis done,—Old things are paft away,   *Heb* 8 13.
And a new State of Things,begun ;   2*Cor* 5.17.
A World whofe Age feels no Decay,   *Heb.* 2. 5,
But fhall out-laft the circling Sun.   6, &c.
                                            *Luke*1.33.
A new Account of Time begins,   *Mat* 26.
When our dear LORD refign'd hisBreath,   28.
Charg'd with our Sorrows and our Sins,
Our Lives to ranfom by his Death.   *Mat.* 20.
                                            28.
Once he was Dead, now lives and reigns   *Rev.*1 18.
Where Angels his Great Deeds proclaim: *Rev.* 5
Let's tell our Joys in pious Strains,   8—14.
And fpread the Glory of his Name.

H Y. M'N L.

[*As the* 100 *Pfalm.*]
THUS we commemorate the Day   *Mat.* 26.
    On which our deareft LORD was flain ;   26,27, 28.
Thus we our pious Homage pay,
Till he appears on Earth again.   1 *Cor.* 11.
                                            26
Come, Dear LORD JESUS, quickly come,   *Rev* 22.20.
Why ftay thy Chariot-Wheels fo long ?
Thy Church below, thy other Home,   15.3 4.
Shall welcome Thee with many a Song.   *Ch.* 19.
                                Come,   4—9.

Rev. 20 11 Come, Great Redeemer, open wide
Rev. 1. 7. The Curtains of the parting Sky:
Pfal. 18. On a bright Cloud in Triumph ride,
9, 10.   And on the Wind's fwift Pinions fly.

Rev 19.16 Come, *King of Kings*, with thy bright Train,
Mat. 25.   Cherubs and Seraphs, Heavenly Hofts,
31.   Affume thy Right, enlarge thy Reign
Phil. 2 9, As far as Earth extends her Coafts.
10, 11.
Phil. 2. 7. Come, LORD, difdain not to come down
      And rule, where thou waft fcorn'd before.
Rev. 5. 9. How well that Head becomes a Crown,
      Which cruel Thorns fo meekly bore!

                          (ftood,
Rev 11. 8. Come, LORD, and where thy Crofs once
Rev. 19.   There plant thy Banner, fix thy Throne;
12, 13,   And ftain the Ground with Rebels Blood,
14, 15.   Which once was purpled with thy own.

Mat. 27.   Come, LORD, what thy weak Reed began,
Pfal. 2 9. Compleat by thy ftrong Iron Rod :
Rev. 2 27. Once Thou wer't feen a *Dying* Man,
Heb. 2. 14. Now fhew thy felf the *Living* GOD.
Rev. 7. 2.

F I N I S.